高等学校商务英语系列教材

总主编　杨翠萍

新编

商务英语听说教程

Business English Listening & Speaking

（第2次修订本）

第1册

学 生 用 书
Student's Book

主　编　周　淳　刘鸣放
副主编　郭　玮　曾凡振　郭　琴
参编者　戴红珍　余　晓　汪玉枝

清华大学出版社

北京交通大学出版社

·北京·

内 容 简 介

本书共 15 个单元，精选了 15 个商务活动中最常用的主题，采用全新的结构，按主题编排各单元的内容，使其更具系统性和可操作性。本书在单元主题的择取和确立上兼顾了社会需求、专业培养目标、学生的认知程度和语言技能，设计了 Preliminary Listening、Listening & Speaking、Further Listening 及 Home Listening 等教学模块，力求突出教材的专业性、商务性及练习的多样性、趣味性和实用性等特点。

本书可供高等学校经贸类专业及商务英语专业的学生使用，同时也可作为具有相应英语水平的商务工作者及商务英语爱好者的参考书。

图书在版编目（CIP）数据

新编商务英语听说教程学生用书. 第 1 册／周淳，刘鸣放主编. — 修订本. — 北京：清华大学出版社；北京交通大学出版社，2009.9（2022.11 修订）
（高等学校商务英语系列教材／杨翠萍总主编）
ISBN 978-7-81123-550-0

Ⅰ. 新…　Ⅱ. ①周…　②刘…　Ⅲ. 商务-英语-听说教学-高等学校-教材
Ⅳ. H319.9

中国版本图书馆 CIP 数据核字（2009）第 154525 号

新编商务英语听说教程学生用书（第 1 册）
XINBIAN SHANGWU YINGYU TINGSHUO JIAOCHENG XUESHENG YONGSHU（DI 1 CE）

责任编辑：张利军
出版发行：清 华 大 学 出 版 社　　邮编：100084　电话：010-62776969　http://www.tup.com.cn
　　　　　北京交通大学出版社　　邮编：100044　电话：010-51686414　http://press.bjtu.edu.cn
印　刷　者：北京鑫海金澳胶印有限公司
经　　　销：全国新华书店
开　　　本：185 mm×260 mm　印张：15.25　字数：495 千字
版 印 次：2022 年 11 月第 1 版第 2 次修订　　2022 年 11 月第 7 次印刷
定　　　价：44.00 元

本书如有质量问题，请向北京交通大学出版社质监组反映。对您的意见和批评，我们表示欢迎和感谢。
投诉电话：010-51686043，51686008；传真：010-62225406；E-mail：press@bjtu.edu.cn。

前　言

　　本书是针对高等学校经贸类专业及商务英语专业的学生、具有相应英语水平的商务工作者及英语爱好者编写的基础课系列教材之一。本书突破了传统的教材模式，综合考虑了高等学校经贸类及商务英语专业学生的特点，力求把经贸和商务知识的传授与英语听说技能的培养结合起来。

　　本书从学生的实际水平出发，始终遵循"学用结合，重在运用"的原则。本书循序渐进，通过内容丰富、专业面广、程度适宜、趣味性强的商务材料，促使学生积极参与有关商务实践的听说活动，在提高其口语表达能力的同时，了解商务活动的各个主要环节，拓宽视野，获取新知识。

　　为适应商务英语听说教学紧扣时代脉搏、满足社会需求的发展趋势，本书编写人员在听取和汇总来自语言教学专家、商务专业人士及教学一线的广大师生等多方面的意见及建议的基础上，结合国外相关教学领域最新的研究成果，在内容的编排、材料的选择、题型的设计和结构的完善等方面进行了大量的创新性探索。

　　本书精选商务活动中最常用的主题，采用全新的结构编排教学内容，使其更具系统性和可操作性。本书在单元主题的择取和确立上兼顾了社会需求、专业培养目标、学生的认知程度和语言技能。本书设计了 Preliminary Listening、Listening & Speaking、Further Listening 及 Home Listening 等教学模块，力求突出教材的专业性、商务性及练习的多样性、趣味性和实用性等特点。

　　本书共 15 个单元，按主题编排各单元的教学内容。各单元的基本构成如下。

　　1. Preliminary Listening：该部分以 spot dictation 的形式对单元主题进行概括性的介绍，旨在导入单元主题并让学生对单元主题有初步的认识和了解，激发学生进一步学习的兴趣和积极性。

　　2. Listening & Speaking：该部分为每个单元的主体构成部分，围绕单元主题对学生进行听与说的综合训练。该部分含两个结构基本相同、内容相对独立的教学模块：Section A 和 Section B。每个教学模块均具有其独立的且与单元主题紧密关联的副主题（sub-topic），并配有相关的一揽子听说活动。这样的编排可以实现化整为零、模块交替、听说结合、师生互动，既保证了教学内容的丰富性和多样性，也便于教师根据自身教学的实际需求，灵活机动地组织课堂教学。因此，本书在借鉴国外同类教材先进经验的基础上，更好地兼顾了教学的灵活性和系统性，弥补了通常按主题定单元所编写的教材在教学系统性方面的缺陷。

Section A 和 Section B 主要包含以下内容。

（1）Pre-listening：针对听力材料中出现的热点问题提问，以导入后续的听说活动。

（2）Listening：分成对话（conversation）和语篇（passage）两部分对学生进行针对性较强的听力训练。对话部分和语篇部分分别配有两项练习，一项侧重培养学生捕捉细节信息的能力，另一项侧重培养学生对信息进行整体把握和综合归纳的技能。

（3）Speaking：围绕教学模块的副主题（sub-topic）设计的综合性的口语活动。活动的形式多样，有小组讨论、看图说话、班级辩论、个案讨论、角色扮演等，旨在培养学生对英语语言和本单元所涉及的商务文化背景知识的综合运用能力。

3. Further Listening：该部分按照特定的商务场景编排了相互关联的 5 个短篇（如电话留言、语音信息、财经新闻简报等）听力练习，帮助学生进一步熟悉真实场景下的商务活动及办公用语。

4. Home Listening：该部分安排了相关的财经新闻报道一篇，突出了商务英语的时效性和在日常生活中的实用性。

本书是以 6 学时完成一个单元为基础来编写的，教师也可根据学生的实际情况灵活使用。

本书以二维码的形式向读者提供音频、听力材料原文、相关背景知识及习题参考答案和解析等教学资源，读者可先扫描书后的防盗码获得资源读取权限，然后再扫描书中每单元开始处的二维码来获取各个单元中每一模块的教学资源。

虽然本书是在全体参编教师多年的教学实践与研究的基础上产生的，但仍可能存在不妥之处和有待进一步完善的地方，欢迎各位专家、同仁及使用本书的广大师生批评指正。

编　者

2022 年 11 月

目录 Contents

Unit **1**

• Telephoning

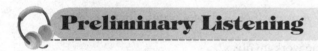
Dictation

Listen to the following short paragraph and fill in the blanks with what you hear.

Probably no means of communication has revolutionized the (1) _____ of people more than the telephone. (2) _____, it is a system that converts sound, specifically the human voice, to (3) _____ of various frequencies and then back to a tone that sounds like the (4) _____. In our hi-tech world of computers and laser printers, the telephone is still most businesses' (5) _____ with customers. Clearly, the telephone is not a business tool to be (6) _____. Just like in a (7) _____, the rules of etiquette in telephone conversations may help make the communication (8) _____ for all those involved.

Listening & Speaking

SECTION A   Handling Office Calls

Pre-listening ▶▶▶

Discussion

• •

Discuss the following questions with your partner and take notes when necessary.

1. What do you think a secretary's routine work involves?

_____

_____

2. What qualities and skills are required for an office secretary?

_____

_____

Listening ▶▶▶

Conversation

• •

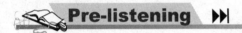

WORD BANK

schedule	/ˈskedʒuəl/	v.	（时间的）预定，安排

candidate	/'kændɪdeɪt/	*n.*	候选人
preferably	/'prefərəblɪ/	*ad.*	最好，更可取地
spaceship	/'speɪʃɪp/	*n.*	太空船
available	/ə'veɪləb(ə)l/	*a.*	可接受探访的，可见客人的

I. Listen to the conversation and choose the best answers to the questions you hear.

1. A. In the early morning.
   C. In the early afternoon.
   B. In the late morning.
   D. In the late afternoon.

2. A. Because he is on another phone line.
   C. Because he is at a production meeting.
   B. Because he is out for an appointment.
   D. Because he is at a job interview.

3. A. To make an appointment with Mr. Simon.
   B. To talk about a new toy design with Mr. Simon.
   C. To apply for the position of Chief Designer.
   D. To discuss the toy production with Mr. Simon.

4. A. To put him through.
   C. To reschedule an appointment for him.
   B. To check if her boss is available.
   D. To ask her boss to return his call.

5. A. Before 4:00 that afternoon.
   C. Before 4:30 that afternoon.
   B. After 4:00 that afternoon.
   D. After 4:30 that afternoon.

II. Listen to the conversation again and complete the phone message below.

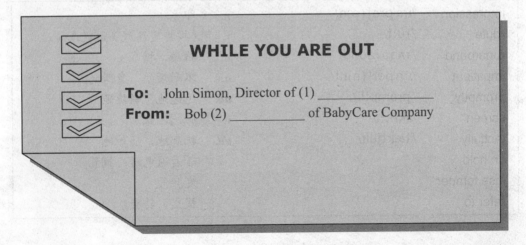

WHILE YOU ARE OUT

To: John Simon, Director of (1) _____
From: Bob (2) _____ of BabyCare Company

MESSAGE

He called about (3) _____

_____

He can be reached on (4) _____ before 4:30 pm

and on (5) _____ after that.

Passage

WORD BANK

impression	/ɪmˈpreʃ(ə)n/	*n.*	印象
route	/ruːt/	*v.*	（按特定路线）运送或传送
runaround	/ˈrʌnəˌraʊnd/	*n.*	推诿，搪塞
impatient	/ɪmˈpeɪʃ(ə)nt/	*a.*	不耐烦的，急躁的
promptly	/ˈprɒmptlɪ/	*ad.*	迅速地，敏捷地
screen	/skriːn/	*v.*	筛选，甄别
tactfully	/ˈtæktfulɪ/	*ad.*	机智地，巧妙地
on hold			等着通电话；搁置
lose temper			发脾气
refer to			提交，转交

I. Listen to the passage and choose the best answer to complete each of the following statements.

1. _____ is thought to be the most difficult and important part of a secretary's work.
   A. Typing letters
   B. Handling office calls
   C. Preparing documents
   D. Receiving visitors

2. The first impression a client receives about a business is often through _____.
   A. a telephone contact
   B. its publicizing materials
   C. a talk with the office secretary
   D. its interior decoration

3. As a good secretary, you should do all the following EXCEPT _____.
   A. answer all phone calls promptly and efficiently
   B. know who is the right person to handle the call
   C. transfer all phone calls to your boss dutifully
   D. keep calm if a caller gets impatient or becomes angry

4. An office secretary who can _____ is a valuable asset to any organization.
   A. deal with "problem" visitors tactfully
   B. handle paper work skillfully and efficiently
   C. speak several foreign languages fluently
   D. handle phone calls cheerfully, tactfully and efficiently

5. To handle a telephone call well is important to a business because _____.
   A. a well-handled phone call will improve its office efficiency
   B. a well-handled phone call will enhance its prestige
   C. a well-handled phone call will boost its market share
   D. a well-handled phone call will leave the caller a good impression

II. Listen to the passage again and complete the notes with what you hear.

Dealing with Office Phone Calls

A Good Secretary Should:

✎ route the call directly to (1) _____.
✎ answer all phone calls (2) _____.

新编 商务英语听说教程 学生用书

- be (3) _____, no matter how busy she is or what kind of mood she may be in.
- (4) _____ if a caller gets impatient or becomes angry.
- know how to (5) _____ telephone calls, i.e., know which calls to refer to (6) _____, which calls to refer to other people, and which calls to (7) _____.

A Good Secretary Should Not:

- leave the caller hanging (8) _____.
- answer the call (9) _____.
- allow herself to (10) _____.

Speaking ▶▶

Discussion & Role-play

☎ Work in groups. Read the following telephone conversation carefully and discuss within the group alternative ways of responding to the caller.

☎ Work in groups. Role-play your improved conversation.

A man calls about keyboards that he ordered but has not yet received. He does not know exactly who to speak to and is being transferred from one department to another.

Secretary:	Hello, ABC Company.	Is this greeting complete?
		_____
		_____
Customer:	Is this ABC Company?	
Secretary:	That's what I said.	What should she have said?
		_____

Customer:	Hello, I'm calling about some keyboards I ordered about a month ago and haven't received yet. I was wondering if you could tell me who I should speak to.	
Secretary:	It's probably Shipping's fault. It usually is.	What's wrong here?
Customer:	Do you think you could…	What should she have said?
Secretary:	Hold.	
Shipping Clerk:	Alfred here.	
Customer:	Is this Shipping?	
Shipping Clerk:	Yeah, what do you want?	How would you replace this?
Customer:	My name is Kevin Smith and I haven't received an order for keyboards that I placed about a month ago.	
Shipping Clerk:	You got your invoice number?	How should he have asked this?
Customer:	No. I never got one.	
Shipping Clerk:	Well, there's nothing I can do to help you. I'll transfer you to Accounting.	Did he forget something here?
Customer:	No, wait, wait! This is long distance.	
Accountant:	Accounting. Who do you want to speak to?	What is the customer's reaction going to be?

SECTION B   Business Phone Etiquette

Discussion

• •

Discuss the following questions with your partner and take notes when necessary.

1. What will you do if the following situations occur while you are making a phone call?

Situations	What you will do
If you are not the person the caller wants to speak to	
If you are connected to an answering machine	
If you are put on hold and have to wait for a connection	
If you get a wrong number	
If the person you are calling is away at the moment	
If the person you are calling is busy at the moment	

2. What rules of telephone etiquette do you happen to know?

Listening ▶▶|

Conversation

WORD BANK

extension	/ɪkˈstenʃ(ə)n/	*n.*	电话分机
personnel	/ˌpɜːsəˈnel/	*n.*	人事部
consult	/kənˈsʌlt/	*v.*	咨询
surname	/ˈsɜːneɪm/	*n.*	姓
confirm	/kənˈfɜːm/	*v.*	确认
participant	/pɑːˈtɪsɪpənt/	*n.*	参与者
urgent	/ˈɜːdʒənt/	*a.*	紧急的

I. Listen to the conversation and complete the phone summary below.

Incoming Phone Call Summary

9:15 Call One

🖊 Call description:

Victoria Baker of M&M Advertising called extension (1) _____.

🖊 Why could not the recipient answer the call?

(2) _____.

🖊 How was the phone call handled?

(3) _____.

10:25 Call Two

🖊 Call description:

Robin Hunter from (4) _____ returned Nancy Foster's call.

✎ Why could not the recipient answer the call?

(5) _____.

✎ How was the phone call handled?

(6) _____.

14:35   *Call Three*

✎ Call Description:

Rose (7) _____ from the INEX Consulting called William Thomson

of (8) _____ Department.

✎ Why could not the recipient answer the call?

(9) _____.

✎ How was the phone call handled?

(10) _____.

II. Listen to the conversation again and complete the phone message below.

PHONE MESSAGE

Message for: *William Thomson*

Name of Caller: *Rose Hobson*

Company: *the INEX Consulting*

MESSAGE:

✎ She called about (1) _____.

✎ She has confirmed (2) _____.

✎ She said she could only take (3) _____

_____.

✎ She asked you to (4) _____.

Passage

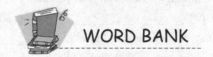

WORD BANK

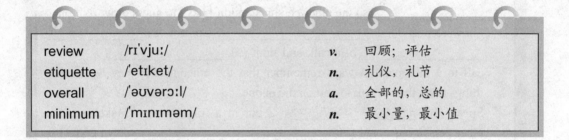

review	/rɪˈvjuː/	v.	回顾；评估
etiquette	/ˈetɪket/	n.	礼仪，礼节
overall	/ˈəʊvərɔːl/	a.	全部的，总的
minimum	/ˈmɪnɪməm/	n.	最小量，最小值

I. Listen to the passage and decide whether the following statements are true or false. Write T for true and F for false in the brackets.

1. (　　) Maria Bush is the manager of Human Resources Department.
2. (　　) Maria Bush is addressing all the company employees on telephone etiquette.
3. (　　) Maria Bush is talking about the importance of telephone in business activities.
4. (　　) According to Maria Bush, a business phone call should be answered promptly.
5. (　　) You are advised to identify yourself immediately when you make or answer a business phone call.
6. (　　) You are advised to have some small talk with your listener before going to the point.
7. (　　) You should ask the caller to call later if you must take another call or do some other work.
8. (　　) It is suggested that you should call other people at the time convenient to them.

II. Listen to the passage again and complete the following telephone etiquette checklist with what you hear.

Telephone Etiquette Checklist

✎ Whenever possible, try to answer your phone by (1) _____. Do not let the phone (2) _____ — doing so will most certainly annoy your caller. Answering calls quickly is (3) _____.

✎ State (4) _____ and (5) _____ in the company immediately when you place or answer a call. Say right away (6) _____ _____, so the other person shouldn't have to guess or work it out.

✎ Show respect for (7) _____. Control (8) _____ _____ of a call, and limit (9) _____ of the call to a minimum. Always remember that the other person may have other things to do than to talk to you on the phone.

✎ Speak (10) _____, but in a friendly way. Make sure the other person has noted (11) _____ down correctly, especially (12) _____.

✎ Do not put someone on hold for (13) _____ or so. If for some important reason you feel you must take another call or do some other work, offer to (14) _____ rather than keep him or her on hold.

✎ Always be polite. Remember to say "(15) _____" and "(16) _____" whenever appropriate. Don't be rude and (17) _____ while on the phone. Give your listener (18) _____.

✎ If possible, don't phone during the other person's (19) _____ or just before (20) _____. You'd better find out what time it is in the other country before you call.

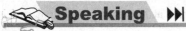

Speaking ▶▶

Role-play

• •

☎ **Work in pairs. You and your partner read each other's activity sheet respectively.**

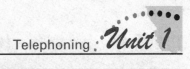

☎ **Work in pairs. Act out the situations with your partner accordingly.**

Activity Sheet for Student A

Situation 1

You have an appointment with Fiona Scott of General Motors on 14 July at noon.
Call her to:

✎ confirm the date.
✎ change the time to 1:45 pm.
✎ bring the new catalogue to the meeting.

Situation 2

You are a receptionist at Sun Chemicals, a company based in New York. Someone calls to speak to George Hunter. He is not in the office at the moment. Offer to take a message.

PHONE MESSAGE

Message for: _____

Name of Caller: _____

Company: _____

MESSAGE:

_____

_____

_____

Activity Sheet for Student B

Situation 1

You are a receptionist at General Motors. Someone calls to speak to Fiona Scott. She is at a meeting at the moment. Offer to take a message.

PHONE   MESSAGE

Message for: _____

Name of Caller: _____

Company: _____

MESSAGE:

_____

_____

_____

Situation 2

You are flying to New York to visit George Hunter at a company called Sun Chemicals. Call him to:

- say that your flight lands at Kennedy International Airport at 9:30 on Wednesday 25 June.
- confirm the flight number: PA 349.
- ask who will meet you at the airport.

Further Listening

Short Recordings

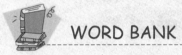 WORD BANK

redundant	/rɪˈdʌndənt/		*a.*	过剩的,多余的
take on				雇用

I. In this section, you will hear five short recordings. For each piece, decide which problem at work the speaker is talking about.

Item 1. ....

Item 2. ....

Item 3. ....

Item 4. ....

Item 5. ....

A. over-staffing

B. an unfair dismissal

C. inadequate training

D. too many changes

E. poor time-keeping

F. low job satisfaction

G. a lack of leadership

H. inadequate safety procedures

II. Listen to the five recordings again and answer the following questions with what you hear.

1. What is said to be the reason for Sam's dismissal according to the first speaker?

_____

2. Why was the second speaker dissatisfied with her current job?

_____

3. What was the third speaker's responsibility when he started off as a trainee in that office?

_____

4. According to the fourth speaker, how will Susan react to what happened to her?

_____

5. What will happen if the company can't win new orders in the next few months?

_____

Home Listening

Business News

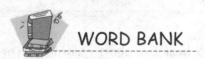 WORD BANK

Census Bureau	（美国）人口调查局
National Retail Federation	美国零售联盟（系美国顶尖零售商组织，提供行业新闻、杂志、联系信息等）
Conference Board	世界大型企业联合会（成立于 1916 年的世界著名商业论坛机构，总部位于纽约，系非赢利组织）
Consumer Confidence Index	消费者信心指数
Commerce Department	（美国）商务部
Dow Jones Industrial Average	（美国）道琼斯工业平均指数

Listen to the business news report and complete the following sentences with what you hear.

1. Consumers produce about _____ of the economic activity in the United States,

much of which takes place during the _____.

2. For big department stores, _____ account for about _____ of their total sales and are almost _____ for the rest of the year.

3. The busiest shopping day of the year used to be the_____, but in recent years the busiest day has been the _____.

4. Being "in the black" means a good thing, a return to profit because storekeepers used to record _____.

5. Another choice for people who do not like crowded stores is _____ and Americans bought almost _____ worth of goods online in the last three months of last year.

6. The National Retail Federation expected holiday sales of about _____ _____, an increase by _____ over last year.

7. The Conference Board reported an increase of _____ in its Consumer Confidence Index, but that is still _____ lower than the starting level of one-hundred set in _____.

8. The report issued by the Commerce Department boosted the Dow Jones Industrial Average to _____ for the first time _____ although the consumer confidence report released by the University of Michigan showed _____ in current conditions.

Unit 2

• Career

🎧 Preliminary Listening

Dictation

•••

Listen to the following short paragraph and fill in the blanks with what you hear.

As the idea of (1) _____ picks up in the 21st century, aided by the power of the Internet and the increased acceptance of people (2) _____, the concept of a career is shifting and in its broadest sense, career refers to (3) _____ over their lifespan. Now that the job-for-life covenant between employer and employee has been superseded by an (4) _____ _____, career management has become a necessary survival skill rather than being an activity pursued by Ivy League alumni or people (5) _____ _____. Job security is now based on (6) _____ rather than (7) _____ to an employer. Career management is nothing more than a small investment of time, money and energy to protect (8) _____ — one's job.

Listening & Speaking

| SECTION A | **Career Management** |

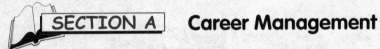

Pre-listening ▶▶

Discussion

· ·

Discuss the following questions with your partner and take notes when necessary.

1. What do your parents do? How do you like their jobs?

....

....

2. Have you ever thought of your future career?

Yes. Then ...	No. Then ...
❏ What do you want to do when you graduate from college?	❏ What careers are you interested in?
❏ What do your parents think of your choice of career?	❏ How will your parents' attitude influence your choice of career?
❏ How will you prepare for your future career?	❏ How can you find out which career is right for you?

Listening ▶▶

Conversation

· ·

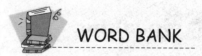

WORD BANK

representative	/ˌreprɪˈzentətɪv/	*n.*	代表
target	/ˈtɑːgɪt/	*n.*	指标，定额
trying	/ˈtraɪɪŋ/	*a.*	难堪的，难受的
subsidiary	/səbˈsɪdɪərɪ/	*a.*	附属的
annual	/ˈænjʊəl/	*a.*	每年的，年度的
Managing Director			总经理
sales representative			销售代表
chain store			连锁商店

I. Listen to the conversation and choose the best answers to the questions you hear.

1. A. Working in the office.　　　　B. Visiting company branches.
   C. Meeting sales representatives.　D. Making business trips abroad.

2. A. He'd report it to the Managing Director and tell him what action he'd take.
   B. He'd meet the sales representatives and discuss the sales figures with them.
   C. He'd visit the branch and talk to the Branch Manager about it.
   D. He'd contact purchasing managers from certain big retailers.

3. A. Weekly.　　　　B. Monthly.
   C. Quarterly.　　　D. Annually.

4. A. His company has never failed to meet its yearly sales target.
   B. His company has difficulty in reaching this year's sales target.
   C. His company missed its yearly sales target on a few occasions.
   D. His company set a sales target too high to achieve this year.

5. A. Mr. Mason deals directly with all his clients himself.
   B. Mr. Mason's company has overseas subsidiary companies.
   C. Mr. Mason spends most of his time visiting branches and traveling abroad.
   D. Mr. Mason has to report to the Branch Managers sometimes.

II. Listen to the conversation again and complete the notes with what you hear.

Activities		Frequency
❑ deal with _____		always
❑ _____		usually
❑ meet _____		quite often
❑ _____		occasionally
❑ visit _____		sometimes
❑ report to _____		every day
❑ meet _____		twice a week
❑ check _____		monthly
❑ prepare _____		quarterly
❑ fix _____		once a year
❑ annual sales figures _____		never

Passage

WORD BANK

counselor	/ˈkaʊnsələ(r)/	n.	顾问
potential	/pəˈtenʃ(ə)l/	n.	潜能，潜力
dynamic	/daɪˈnæmɪk/	a.	有生气的，精力充沛的
attorney	/əˈtɜːnɪ/	n.	〈美〉辩护律师
concentration	/ˌkɒnsənˈtreɪʃ(ə)n/	n.	集中，专心
once in a lifetime			千载难逢的，一生只有一次的

I. Listen to the passage and choose the best answers to the questions you hear.

1. A. To assist companies to find the most qualified employees.

   B. To offer people his advice on how to choose the right career.

   C. To train people with the potential to become writers or businesspeople.

   D. To help people exploit their strengths to achieve success in job-hunting.

2. A. A writer.   B. A lawyer.   C. A counselor.   D. A businessman.

3. A. Creativity.   B. Concentration.   C. Hard work.   D. All of the above.

4. A. The new job is poorly paid.

   B. The working hours are too long.

   C. The office is far away from her home.

   D. The new job might affect her family life.

5. A. Juliet is in two minds about taking a more responsible job.

   B. Juliet worked as a secretary in a law office before she got married.

   C. If Bob takes the new job, he has to work abroad alone for three years.

   D. Bob is excited about the prospect of living and working in a foreign country.

II. Listen to the passage again and answer the following questions with what you hear.

1. What is David Wright's advice on how to choose the right career?

   _____

   _____

2. What are the basic personalities required for a potential businessperson?

   _____

3. What was Juliet's former job? Why did she quit?

   _____

   _____

4. What's Bob's new job? How does he like it?

   _____

   _____

5. Why does not Bob's company encourage its employees to take their families while working abroad?

   _____

   _____

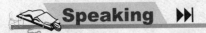 **Speaking** ▶▶|

Discussion & Role-play

Thinking about a career is always hard for youngsters. It will help you to make a smart career choice if you know your unique qualities — your abilities, talents, needs, values, and interests. Here is a quiz to help you learn more about yourself.

☎ **Work alone. Read each statement in the quiz below and decide if it describes you.**

Personality Quiz

What I like

1. I like to work with animals, tools, or machines.
   ☺ True   ☺ Mostly True   ☹ Not true

2. I like to study and solve math or science problems.
   ☺ True   ☺ Mostly True   ☹ Not true

3. I like to do creative activities like art, drama, crafts, dance, music, or creative writing.
   ☺ True   ☺ Mostly True   ☹ Not true

4. I like to do things where I can help people — like, teaching, first aid, or giving information.
   ☺ True   ☺ Mostly True   ☹ Not true

5. I like to lead and persuade people, and to sell things and ideas.
   ☺ True   ☺ Mostly True   ☹ Not true

6. I like to work with numbers, records, or machines in a set, orderly way.
   ☺ True   ☺ Mostly True   ☹ Not true

How I see myself

1. I am practical, mechanical, and realistic.
   ☺ True   ☺ Mostly True   ☹ Not true

---

2. I am precise, scientific, and intellectual.
   ☺ True   ☺ Mostly True   ☹ Not true
3. I am artistic, imaginative, original, and independent.
   ☺ True   ☺ Mostly True   ☹ Not true
4. I am helpful, friendly, and trustworthy.
   ☺ True   ☺ Mostly True   ☹ Not true
5. I am energetic, ambitious, and sociable.
   ☺ True   ☺ Mostly True   ☹ Not true
6. I am orderly, and good at following a set plan.
   ☺ True   ☺ Mostly True   ☹ Not true

What I value

1. I value practical things you can see and touch like plants and animals you can grow, or things you can build or make better.
   ☺ True   ☺ Mostly True   ☹ Not true
2. I value the creative arts — like drama, music, art, or the works of creative writers.
   ☺ True   ☺ Mostly True   ☹ Not true
3. I value helping people and solving social problems.
   ☺ True   ☺ Mostly True   ☹ Not true
4. I value success in politics, leadership, or business.
   ☺ True   ☺ Mostly True   ☹ Not true
5. I value science.
   ☺ True   ☺ Mostly True   ☹ Not true

☎ **Work in pairs. Share your findings about yourself with your partner and describe what type of people your partner is in your eyes.**

☎ **Work in groups. Suppose you are a would-be employee trying to figure out where you belong and the other students in the group are occupation counselors. After reading your quiz results and considering your skills and interests, the counselors suggest some work possibilities for you. Take turns to play the role of a counselee and that of a counselor with the help of your activity sheets.**

Activity Sheet for Counselor

You may choose some of the following questions or ask whatever you think necessary to find out more about your counselee:

- ❏ What do you like to do?
- ❏ What are you good at?
- ❏ What do you expect of the job?
- ❏ Do you like physical or outdoor activities?
- ❏ Do you mind traveling a lot?
- ❏ Are you patient with children or the elderly?

Activity Sheet for Counselee

You may choose some of the following questions or ask whatever you think necessary to have a clearer picture about the career in question:

- ❏ What do people exactly do at work?
- ❏ Is the job interesting or rather boring?
- ❏ What are the skills or knowledge required for this job?
- ❏ What is the responsibility of the job?
- ❏ What future prospects does this job offer?
- ❏ Does the job require a lot of contact with the public or co-workers?

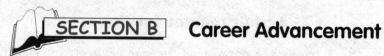

SECTION B Career Advancement

Pre-listening ▶▶

Discussion

Discuss the following questions with your partner and take notes when necessary.

1. What is important for you in a job? And why?

2. Why do you think people choose to job-hop?

Listening ▶▶

Conversation

WORD BANK

| irritating | /ˈɪrɪteɪtɪŋ/ | a. | 气人的，使人不愉快的 |

outnumber	/ˌaʊtˈnʌmbə(r)/	v.	数目超过，比……多
query	/ˈkwɪərɪ/	n.	询问
recompense	/ˈrekəmpens/	v.	补偿，回报
administrator	/ədˈmɪnɪstreɪtə(r)/	n.	行政人员
correspondence	/ˌkɒrɪˈspɒnd(ə)ns/	n.	信件，函件
all walks of life			各行各业
in some measure			多少，稍稍

I. Listen to the conversation and choose the best answers to the questions you hear.

1. A. Her boss is very irritating.

   B. She is poorly paid.

   C. She doesn't get along well with her colleagues.

   D. She has to deal with annoying people sometimes.

2. A. Receiving incoming visitors.

   B. Answering queries from customers.

   C. Responding to faxes.

   D. Scheduling business meetings.

3. A. His job is very demanding.

   B. He has to work overtime.

   C. He is underpaid.

   D. He has to travel a lot.

4. A. Sarah is satisfied with her current employment.

   B. Sarah's job is demanding but very rewarding.

   C. Sarah desires to take more responsibility in her job.

   D. Sarah is eager to get a promotion as well as a pay rise.

5. A. Joan doesn't enjoy meeting people because they are irritating.

   B. Paul spends most of his time visiting shops and customers abroad.

   C. Sarah is looking forward to a job more responsible and demanding.

   D. Paul's company rewards its employees with free trips to foreign countries.

II. Listen to the conversation again and complete the personnel files below.

---

1) Personal File
Joan London

Job: _____

Responsibilities:
☐ Dealing with _____
☐ Sending _____

What she enjoys about the job:

What she does not enjoy about the job:
_____

---

2) Personal File
Paul Haywood

Job: _____

Responsibilities:
☐ Visiting _____
☐ Answering _____
☐ Studying _____
☐ Planning _____

What he enjoys about the job:
_____

What he does not enjoy about the job:
_____

3) Personal File
Sarah Jones

Job:_____

Responsibilities:
- ❑ Responding to _____
- ❑ Arranging _____
- ❑ Dealing with _____

What she enjoys about the job:
_____

What she does not enjoy about the job:
_____

Passage

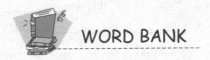

WORD BANK

trait	/treɪt/	*n.*	特征，品质
scholarship	/ˈskɔləʃɪp/	*n.*	学业成绩；学识
initiative	/ɪˈnɪʃɪətɪv/	*n.*	首创（精神），主动性
interchangeability	/ˌɪntə(ː)ˌtʃeɪndʒəˈbɪlɪtɪ/	*n.*	可交换性
inhuman	/ɪnˈhjuːmən/	*a.*	不近人情的，非人道的
seniority	/ˌsiːnɪˈɔrɪtɪ/	*n.*	资历

I. Listen to the passage and decide whether the following statements are true or false. Write T for true and F for false in the brackets.

1. (   ) In the United States, family and education background is the key to personal progress.

2. (   ) Personal advancement in the United States is chiefly based on frequent job-hopping.

3. (   ) Americans consider it inhuman and disloyal to job-hop frequently.

4. (   ) Americans hold that only incapable people will bounce back to work for their original company again.

5. (   ) In the United States, employees are encouraged by their employers to change their jobs frequently.

6. (   ) According to this passage, Americans are a people of high mobility.

7. (   ) Employers in the United States are not happy with the idea of job-hopping because it will cost them a lot to recruit and train the green hands.

8. (   ) The passage is mainly about American attitudes toward personal progress and job-hopping.

II. Listen to the passage again and complete the notes with what you hear.

1. In the United States traits that lead to success are generally considered to be the willingness to work hard, _____, _____, _____ _____.

2. Americans consider it a "right" to be able to _____, to _____ _____, to_____ if they can keep _____ _____.

3. To Americans, new jobs present new _____, new _____, new _____, and new _____ — often a new _____ _____.

Speaking ▶▶▶

Discussion & Debate

Have you ever heard of the saying that a rolling stone gathers no moss? It tells us that a person who too frequently changes his jobs or who never settles in one place will not succeed in life. Does the saying make any sense to you? What is your view on the issue of job-hopping?

☎ **Work in groups. List some positive and negative aspects of job–hopping. Be sure that every one in the group should make his or her contribution.**

Positive Aspects	Negative Aspects

☎ **Work alone. Study the following case carefully and think about what advice you would like to give.**

Case Study

Here printed is a letter written by Angelina to *Just Ask*, a newspaper column designed to publish various problems asked by some troubled readers and advice or suggestions offered by consultants or other readers.

…

I'm an office clerk. Frankly, the pay of my job is good, and it's relaxing. But I really don't like it because I feel it's too boring to bear. And the people around me have nothing to do every day but chat. So I can't learn anything from work. I want to learn some real things while I'm still young, so I have decided to change jobs. But my parents were very angry when they heard this. They think I'm crazy and forbid me to change my job. What should I do?

…

☎ Work as a class. Divide the class into two sides. Side A backs up the girl s decision to job-hop, while Side B is in support of her parents and insists that the girl should not give up her current job at all.

☎ Work in groups. Make groups of four to six students. Half of the groups will take the side of A and the other half will side with B. Have a pre-debate discussion. Each group prepares its arguments and supporting facts by brainstorming together.

☎ Work in groups. Start the debate, which takes place between the two groups holding opposite views and goes on until one side fails to retort.

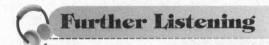

Short Recordings

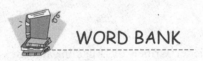

occupation	/ˌɔkjuˈpeɪʃ(ə)n/	n.	（房产等的）占有，居住
guarantee	/ˌgærənˈtiː/	v.	保证
facility	/fəˈsɪlɪtɪ/	n.	（银行）业务
overdraft	/ˈəʊvədrɑːft/	n.	透支；透支额
duration	/djʊəˈreɪʃ(ə)n/	n.	持续时间；期间
premium	/ˈpriːmɪəm/	n.	保险费

I. In this section, you will hear five short recordings. For each piece, decide where each speaker is.

Item 1.   ----------------------
Item 2.   ----------------------
Item 3.   ----------------------
Item 4.   ----------------------
Item 5.   ----------------------

A. bank
B. car hire company
C. credit card company
D. insurance company
E. office letting agency
F. office stationer's
G. parcel carrier office
H. travel agency

II. Listen to the five recordings again and choose the best answers to the questions you hear.

1. A. Refunding the purchaser's money for the damaged boxes.
   B. Replacing the damaged boxes with another two new ones.
   C. Offering a four-percent discount on the purchaser's new order.
   D. Delivering two boxes in stock to the purchaser tomorrow.

2. A. Where the property is located.   B. When the property is available.
   C. What insurance the property carries. D. How the property is maintained.

3. A. Time.   B. Cost.
   C. Safety.   D. Mode of payment.

4. A. $ 5.   B. $ 50.
   C. $ 75.   D. $ 100.

5. A. Royal is a world leading insurance company.
   B. Royal provides a wide range of insurance products.
   C. Royal enjoys a high reputation in the business.
   D. Royal offers very competitive insurance rates.

Home Listening

Business News

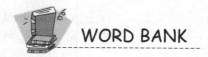

WORD BANK

Securities and Exchange Commission	美国证券交易委员会
National Association of Securities Dealers	美国证券经纪商协会（系规划证券业行为、法规及伦理的一个自我监督机构）
J. P. Morgan Securities	摩根大通证券股份有限公司

Listen to the business news report and answer the following questions with what you hear.

1. What is the Securities and Exchange Commission?

_____

_____

2. What led to the establishment of the Securities and Exchange Commission and when was it established?

_____

_____

3. How many members are there in the commission and what is their job?

_____

_____

4. What are the four divisions of the Securities and Exchange Commission?

_____

_____

5. Why is J. P. Morgan Securities mentioned in the news?

_____

_____

Unit 3

Job Interview

Dictation

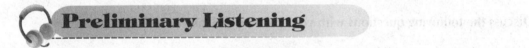

Listen to the following short paragraph and fill in the blanks with what you hear.

A job interview is a process in which (1) _____ is evaluated by an employer for (2) _____ in their company or organization. Interviews are usually preceded by the (3) _____, selecting a small number of candidates who seem to be the most desirable. While job interviews are considered to be one of the (4) _____ for evaluating potential employees, they also demand (5) _____ from the employer. (6) _____ of job interviews may be used where there are many candidates or the job is particularly (7) _____. Once all candidates have had job interviews, the employer typically selects the most desirable candidate and begins the (8) _____ _____ .

Listening & Speaking

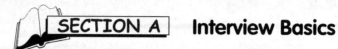

SECTION A   Interview Basics

Pre-listening ▶▶|

Discussion

● ●

Discuss the following questions with your partner and take notes when necessary.

1. What purpose do you think a job interview serves?

The interviewer wants ...	The applicant wants ...
■ to learn whether the applicant has the potential to perform a specific job ■ ■ ■	■ to learn what his or her specific duties and responsibilities will be if hired ■ ■ ■

2. What information do you think a CV (curriculum vitae) or résumé should cover? And does it pay to make your CV or résumé visually appealing? Why and why not?

Listening ▶▶|

Conversation

● ●

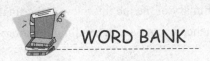

WORD BANK

shortlist	/ˈʃɔːtlɪst/	n.	供最后挑选用的候选人名单
appointee	/əˌpɔɪnˈtiː/	n.	被任命者
neutral	/ˈnjuːtrəl/	a.	无确定性质的
biographically	/ˌbaɪəˈɡræfɪkəlɪ/	ad.	传记体地
elicit	/ɪˈlɪsɪt/	v.	探出，诱出
concrete	/ˈkɔnkriːt/	a.	具体的
sketch out			简略地描述
settle down			定下心来

I. Listen to the conversation and choose the best answers to the questions you hear.

1. A. Contacted the candidates on the shortlist about the timing of the interviews.

   B. Sent the letters of job interview invitation to the candidates on the shortlist.

   C. Conducted the first round of interviews with candidates over the telephone.

   D. Confirmed the interview arrangements with the candidates on the shortlist.

2. A. General Manager. B. Personnel Manager.

   C. Sales Manager. D. Current Advertising Supervisor.

3. A. To introduce the interviewers to the interviewee.

   B. To describe roughly the plan of interview.

   C. To elicit basic information about the interviewee.

   D. To explain briefly the decision-making process.

4. A. The newly-appointed Advertising Supervisor will work closely with Sam's Department.

   B. Sylvia will observe the candidate's behavior with Sam focusing on the answers at the interview.

   C. Sam is recommended to organize the second stage of the interview alphabetically.

   D. Sylvia will have a neutral chat with the interviewee in order to show a casual image.

5. A. Sylvia will run the interview as she is higher in rank than Sam.

B. Sylvia has the final say in deciding whom to hire.

C. Sylvia will do the summary of the job interview at the final stage.

D. Sylvia is more experienced than Sam in handling job interviews.

II. Listen to the conversation again and complete the notes with what you hear.

HOW TO RUN A JOB INTERVIEW	
The position offered: (1) _____	
Interviewer: Sylvia — (2) _____ Sam — Sales Manager	
Time for interview: (3) _____	
Interview Stage	Interview Activities
The First Stage	✎ Introducing ✎ Having a neutral chat — travel, weather, and things of that sort. ✎ Sketching out (4) _____ to ■ help (5) _____ ■ show (6) _____ ✎ To explain (7) _____ briefly
The Second Stage	✎ Asking questions following a structure ■ biographically organized — (8) _____ _____ ■ based on (9) _____ — experience relevant to the job ■ to start with questions dealing with (10) _____ _____ ✎ Listening to the answers ✎ Observing (11) _____ ✎ Answering questions arising in the course of interview
The Final Stage	✎ Summarizing the interview — to cover the main points ✎ Inviting final questions ✎ Saying (12) _____

Passage

WORD BANK

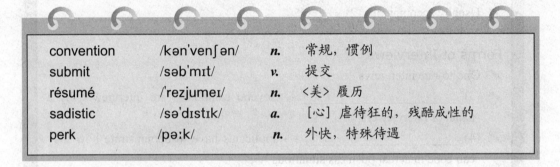

convention	/kən'venʃən/	*n.*	常规，惯例
submit	/səb'mɪt/	*v.*	提交
résumé	/'rezjumeɪ/	*n.*	<美> 履历
sadistic	/sə'dɪstɪk/	*a.*	[心] 虐待狂的，残酷成性的
perk	/pə:k/	*n.*	外快，特殊待遇

I. Listen to the passage and decide whether the following statements are true or false. Write T for true and F for false in the brackets.

1. (   ) A letter of application will include all the unchanging information about the applicant.

2. (   ) Conventions applying to the process of job application and interviews vary from country to country.

3. (   ) A neatly typed CV and application letter will give the interviewer a better impression of the candidate.

4. (   ) The traditional one-to-one interview is thought to be a bit out of fashion these days.

5. (   ) Generally, the atmosphere at panel interviews tends to be more formal than that at one-to-one interviews.

6. (   ) At deep-end interviews, applicants are required to show their capability to deal with actual business situations.

7. (   ) Since fashions change quite rapidly in interview techniques, there are many rules highly recommendable to applicants.

8. (   ) How much the job pays may not be the only consideration while weighing a job offer.

II. Listen to the passage again and complete the notes with what you hear.

Job Application & Interviews

About CV
✎ Contains all the unchanging information about the applicant: (1) _____

_____

✎ Usually accompanies (2) _____

Forms of Interviews
✎ One-to-one interviews
✎ (3) _____ — several candidates are interviewed by a
panel of interviewers
✎ (4) _____ — applicants have to demonstrate how they
can cope in actual business situations

Atmosphere of Interviews
✎ Varies from the informal to the formal and from kindly to sadistic

Rules to Be Aware of
✎ (5) "_____"
✎ (6) "_____"

Perks Contributive to Job Attractiveness
✎ a company car
✎ (7) _____
✎ (8) _____
✎ (9) _____
✎ generous holidays
✎ (10) _____

Speaking ▶▶|

Discussion

• •

☎ **Work in groups. Discuss how you would feel and what exactly you would say or do in each of the following situations during an interview for a job that you are eager to get.**

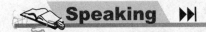

> 🖉 You are still waiting for the interview to begin an hour after the appointed time.
>
> 🖉 The interviewer has not prepared for the interview: he or she does not seem to have read your CV or application letter.
>
> 🖉 The interviewer never looks you straight in the eye.
>
> 🖉 The interviewer's mobile phone rings again and again.
>
> 🖉 The room is hot and stuffy and you have a terrible headache.
>
> 🖉 The interviewer is very talkative and keeps interrupting you.
>
> 🖉 At the end of the interview you are still not clear about the nature of the job.
>
> 🖉 The interviewer doesn't mention when you may expect to hear the decision.

☎ **Work as a class. Share your insights with the rest of the class.**

SECTION B Interview Tips

Pre-listening ▶▶

Discussion

Discuss the following questions with your partner and take notes when necessary.

1. What are the typical questions that an interviewer might ask? And how will you respond to those questions?

   _____

   _____

2. How will you prepare for an important job interview?

   _____

   _____

Listening ▶▶

Conversation

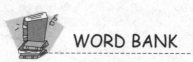

WORD BANK

pertinent	/ˈpəːtɪnənt/	*a.*	相关的

in-service	/ˈɪnˈsəːvɪs/	*a.*	在职的，不脱产的
Michigan	/ˈmɪʃɪɡən/	*n.*	密歇根州（美国州名）
Microsoft			美国微软公司
Word			微软公司研发的文字处理软件
PowerPoint			微软公司研发的制作幻灯片和简报的软件

I. Listen to the conversation and choose the best answers to the questions you hear.

1. A. She received a BA degree in Business Administration.
   B. She received a BA degree in both Marketing and Business Administration.
   C. She received a degree in foreign languages at Michigan State University.
   D. She received all her primary, secondary and higher education in Michigan.

2. A. From her mother.
   B. Through correspondence courses.
   C. Through in-service training.
   D. Through her university studies.

3. A. By fax.   B. By phone.
   C. By e-mail.   D. By correspondence.

4. A. She hopes for career advancement.
   B. She is underpaid at the present job.
   C. The current position is too demanding for her.
   D. The current job does not offer traveling opportunities.

5. A. The interviewee left both her home and mobile phone number on her application form.
   B. The interviewee needs to use Microsoft Office applications in her current secretarial work.
   C. The interviewee has changed her work several times in the hope of more promotion opportunities.
   D. The interviewee does not mind working overtime and doing a lot of business traveling.

II. Listen to the conversation again and complete the interview minutes with what you hear.

SUNRISE COMPUTER		
Position applied for	(1) _____	
Interviewer	Paul Johnson, the (2) _____ Manager	
About Interviewee		
Personal Details	Full Name	Betty Smith
	Age	(3) _____
	Sex	Female
	Place of Birth	Michigan
	Marital Status	(4) _____
	Telephone	(5) _____
Higher Education	University	Michigan State University
	Business Courses	Received A's in both (6) _____ _____ and Marketing
	Graduation Time	In (7) _____
Work Experience	Current Employer	Universal Toy Company
	Responsibilities	Secretarial work: typing letters; (8) _____; making appointments for the boss; talking to visitors, etc.
Qualifications	Keyboard Skills	(9) _____ wpm
	Computer Skills	Microsoft Word — for (10)_____ PowerPoint — for (11) _____
	Language Skills	(12) _____ — Fluent (13) _____ — Average
Reason(s) for quitting current job	Hope to find something (14) _____ to do; to receive (15) _____; to have (16) _____ as getting more experienced.	

Remarks: YES   NO
➢ Is the applicant willing to work overtime?   (   )   (   )
➢ Is the applicant free for business travel?   (   )   (   )
➢ Is the applicant's telephone number permanent?   (   )   (   )

Passage

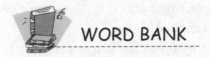

WORD BANK

tip	/tɪp/	n.	秘诀，窍门
flatter	/ˈflætə/	v.	奉承
itemize	/ˈaɪtəmaɪz/	v.	分项开列，逐项列出
illustrate	/ˈɪləstreɪt/	v.	举例说明
justify	/ˈdʒʌstɪfaɪ/	v.	证明……有道理
imprecise	/ˌɪmprɪˈsaɪs/	a.	含糊的
appreciate	/əˈpriːʃɪeɪt/	v.	重视
tolerant	/ˈtɔlərənt/	a.	宽容的

I. Listen to the passage and choose the best answers to the questions you hear.

1. A. To show the applicant how to prepare for a job interview.

   B. To show the applicant how to do his or her best at a job interview.

   C. To show the applicant how to impress interviewers at a job interview.

   D. To show the applicant how to handle tricky questions at a job interview.

2. A. The interviewer and the applicant's previous boss may be birds of a feather（同类的人）.

   B. A man who speaks ill of somebody else in the back is not reliable and trustworthy.

   C. It is highly likely that the interviewer and the applicant's previous boss are acquaintances.

   D. The interviewer may think in this way: if you attack your previous employer now, you might attack your new one too.

3. A. To hold a certain edge（优势）over the interviewer.

   B. To have more chance of demonstrating his or her ability.

C. To learn more about the interviewer's likes and dislikes.

D. To make the interview run in the way in his or her favor.

4. A. The applicant should answer every question raised by the interviewer as thoroughly as possible.

   B. The applicant should accommodate（迁就）the interviewer's expectations and appear to be the sort of person he is looking for.

   C. The applicant should try his or her best to flatter the interviewer and never disagree with him.

   D. It is foolish of the applicant to take the question "Tell me about your strength" as an invitation to chatter.

5. A. Interviewers are always interested in getting as full a picture as possible of the applicant at the interview.

   B. A careful analysis of his or her qualifications and the job descriptions will better prepare the applicant for the forthcoming interview.

   C. The applicant is advised to give more attention to questions such as, "Can you work well in a team or on your own or in a small business?"

   D. Questions such as "Tell me about your strengths" should be treated as an indication that the applicant should talk more about himself or herself.

II. Listen to the passage again and summarize the tips offered by the speaker with your own words.

1. _____

2. _____

3. _____

4. _____

5. _____

 Speaking ▶▶▶

Role-play

☎ **Work as a class. Divide the class into half and role-play a job interview. Half the class will be playing the role of interviewers and the other half as candidates being interviewed. Follow the instructions given in the table and perform the task respectively.**

Interviewers	Candidates
Be divided into 4–6 panels. Each panel decides what job to offer and advertises it on the blackboard or OHP transparency.	Prepare a full CV. You are allowed to invent information about yourself at this stage, but you should stick to it while being interviewed.
Decide how to run the interview: What questions are you going to ask? What personal qualities are you looking for? Are you going to be kind to the candidates or give them a hard time? …	Study the job advertisements carefully. Select one job which most appeals to you and submit your CV to the corresponding panel.
Read the CVs you receive. Decide which candidates look promising and what special questions you'll ask each one.	Consider what questions you are likely to be asked and make sure you know how to answer them while waiting for your turn to be interviewed.
Start the interview with the questions you have prepared. Make notes on each candidate's qualifications or potential under headings such as health, personality, education, training, language proficiency, work experience, working under stress, cooperating with other people, etc.	Answer every question raised by the panel confidently and tactfully. Try to impress the panel. If you are not satisfied with your performance at the interview, you may chance your luck with another panel.
Make brief comments on each candidate you have interviewed and announce your list of successful candidates.	Tell the class your impression of the interviewing panel and what advice you'd like to give them.

Further Listening

Short Recordings

WORD BANK

finalize	/ˈfaɪnəlaɪz/	*v.*	使完成，把……最后定下来
brochure	/brəʊˈʃʊər/	*n.*	小册子
Frankfurt			法兰克福（德国中西部城市）

I. In this section, you will hear five short recordings. For each piece, decide what the speaker is trying to do.

Item 1. ·························

Item 2. ·························

Item 3. ·························

Item 4. ·························

Item 5. ·························

A. make an enquiry

B. offer help

C. cancel an appointment

D. accept an invitation

E. refuse an offer

F. confirm information

G. make a complaint

H. change an order

II. Listen to the five recordings again and decide whether the following statements are true or false. Write T for true and F for false in the brackets.

1. (   ) The first speaker called to confirm the arrangements about Mr. Peterson's visit to the Frankfurt Automobile Fair.

2. (   ) Mr. Peterson will contact Mr. Warren to express his gratitude for the invitation

when he returns from his Chicago trip.

3. (　　) Anna Cooper called to cancel her reservation at the "Executives in the 21st Century" workshop in Shanghai.

4. (　　) Anna Cooper preferred to be called back on 86 021 53289543 if there are any free places at the October workshop.

5. (　　) Brenda would like Paul to go over and have a look at her computer after five that afternoon.

6. (　　) Paul has got an appointment with Brenda at three to check her broken-down computer.

7. (　　) Marie Noble from ERS ordered three thousand copies of the brochure first and then changed her order to four thousand copies.

8. (　　) Marie Noble from ERS offered to call again to confirm the new figure for the copies of the brochure.

9. (　　) James Williams is unable to make the appointment as he has to stay and deal with a serious problem.

10. (　　) James Williams suggests their making another meeting some time later in the week.

Home Listening

Business News

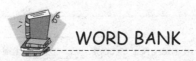

WORD BANK

summit	/ˈsʌmɪt/	*n.*	最高级会议，峰会
clash	/klæʃ/	*n.*	冲突

riot police		防暴警察
Miami	/maɪˈæmɪ/	迈阿密 (美国佛罗里达州东南部港口城市)
Argentina	/ˌɑːdʒənˈtiːnə/	阿根廷 (南美洲国家)
Cuba	/ˈkjuːbə/	古巴 (拉丁美洲国家，首都为哈瓦那)
Caribbean	/ˌkærɪˈbɪ(ː)ən/	加勒比海

Listen to the business news report and complete the answers to the following questions.

1. What happened in Miami, Florida this week?

    A. _____ from North, Central and South American countries gathered in Miami, Florida, this week to _____.

    B. _____ opposed to the Free Trade Area of the Americas clashed with _____ during the talks in Miami this week.

2. What did the Free Trade Area of the Americas aim at?

    The goal was to _____ among member countries. It was also designed to _____ of all people in the area and better _____.

3. What was achieved in the final Friday declaration?

    A greatly reduced plan was agreed upon, which includes a limited number of _____ such as _____. The declaration did not include issues such as _____ and _____. And _____ will now be dealt with by the World Trade Organization.

4. What else do you know about the Free Trade Area of the Americas?

    A. It was first proposed at _____ in Miami in _____. The presidents of the thirty-four democracies in the area agreed to _____ _____ into one free trade area.

    B. If approved, it would create _____ in the world, which includes all the nations in the area except _____ and brings together _____ _____ people from Argentina to Canada.

Unit 4

Office

Preliminary Listening

Dictation

• •

Listen to the following short paragraph and fill in the blanks with what you hear.

All changes in the office were and still are driven by (1) _____
_____. The overwhelming impact of computers on office work has resulted in redesigning the office around, if not for, the computer. In many instances the computers have changed not only (2) _____ and (3) _____, but it has also affected even (4) _____
_____. The future office will be increasingly (5) _____
_____ with core teams managing employees' work from diverse locations — from home offices to temporary business spaces to cafés. A premium will be placed on staff members who possess (6) _____,
and can adapt quickly to change. Professionals able to (7) _____
_____ and (8) _____ will be among the most marketable as innovation continues to drive business.

Listening & Speaking

SECTION A   **Office Work**

Pre-listening ▶▶

Discussion

• •

Discuss the following questions with your partner and take notes when necessary.

1. What do you think is an office clerk's routine work? Do you like to work as an office clerk? Why or why not?

   ----

2. As an employee, do you like to work on flexible working hours? As a boss, would you like to introduce flextime system into the workplace? State your reasons.

Listening ▶▶

Conversation

• •

WORD BANK

photocopy	/ˈfəʊtəʊkɔpɪ/	*v.*	影印

original	/əˈrɪdʒɪn(ə)l/	*n.*	原件
dictate	/dɪkˈteɪt/	*v.*	口授
Dictaphone	/ˈdɪktəfəʊn/	*n.*	录音电话机
transcribe	/trænˈskraɪb/	*v.*	抄录
Xerox	/ˈzɪərɔks/	*v.*	用静电印刷复制
		n.	静电复印机，施乐复印机（商标名称）
reproduction	/ˌriːprəˈdʌkʃ(ə)n/	*n.*	复制，翻印
punch	/pʌntʃ/	*n.*	打孔机
offset	/ˈɔfset/	*n.*	胶印，平版印刷
counter-offer			还价，还盘

I. Listen to the conversation and choose the best answers to the questions you hear.

1. A. Dictated the counter-offer letter.　　B. Signed the counter-offer letter.
   C. Duplicated the counter-offer letter.　　D. Mailed the counter-offer letter.

2. A. Because there is no Xerox machine in the office.
   B. Because the Xerox machine in her office is broken.
   C. Because the Xerox machine in her office is being serviced.
   D. Because she does not know how to operate the Xerox machine.

3. A. To meet the Managing Director.
   B. To input punch cards on the computer.
   C. To have a meeting with the production and marketing staff.
   D. To interview the applicant for the position of chief accountant.

4. A. The Managing Director.　　B. Mr. Jackson.
   C. Mr. Thompson.　　D. Mr. Jefferson.

5. A. Miss Fish will prepare the interview information for her boss.
   B. Miss Fish will arrange for that night's dinner for her boss.
   C. Miss Fish will compose a staff meeting speech for her boss.
   D. Miss Fish will calculate the budget figures for her boss.

II. Listen to the conversation again and mark out the jobs that Miss Fish, the secretary,

is going to do with an F, and that Mr. Main, the boss, is going to do with an M in the brackets. Leave the tasks that have already been performed by either Miss Fish or Mr. Main unmarked.

1. (   ) To type, sign and photocopy the counter-offer letter to the German company.
2. (   ) To dictate two letters on the Dictaphone.
3. (   ) To transcribe the two letters dictated on the Dictaphone.
4. (   ) To mail the original of the counter-offer letter and keep the copy for file.
5. (   ) To take some material to the reproduction department to be Xeroxed.
6. (   ) To Answer Mr. Jackson's phone call.
7. (   ) To call Mr. Jackson back.
8. (   ) To input punch cards on the computer.
9. (   ) To calculate a list of figures for the budget.
10. (   ) To prepare the speech for a meeting with the production and marketing staff.
11. (   ) To have a meeting with the production and marketing staff.
12. (   ) To deliver some documents as marked.
13. (   ) To meet the Managing Director about the advertising budget.
14. (   ) To send a leaflet for the offset print.
15. (   ) To book a table at Madison Restaurant.
16. (   ) To call a client, telling him the nearest route to Madison and reminding him to bring some samples for his appointment.
17. (   ) To get the applicant's information pack ready before the interview.
18. (   ) To interview the applicant for the position of Chief Accountant.
19. (   ) To have a business dinner with a client.

Passage

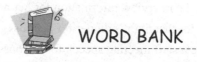

WORD BANK

| philosophy | /fɪˈlɒsəfɪ/ | *n.* | 人生观 |

flexible	/ˈfleksɪb(ə)l/	*a.*	灵活的
hierarchical	/ˌhaɪəˈrɑːkɪk(ə)l/	*a.*	分等级的
establishment	/ɪˈstæblɪʃmənt/	*n.*	机构
tease	/tiːz/	*v.*	取笑，逗弄

I. Listen to the passage and decide whether the following statements are true or false. Write T for true and F for false in the brackets.

1. (   )　American employees tend to work hard only in the presence of the boss.

2. (   )　In America, employees can handle their office hours at their pleasure if they have completed their work.

3. (   )　Employees in America are expected to work through the lunch hour or take work home at night.

4. (   )　Bosses in the States usually work even harder than their employees.

5. (   )　The system of flexible working hours is very common now in the USA as it can keep traffic and commuting problems down.

6. (   )　Working on flexible schedules, career women can spend more time with their families.

7. (   )　In the States people will almost never be fired when they have once got a job, unless they do something awful.

8. (   )　In America, the staff are not allowed to talk to one another during the office hours.

II. Listen to the passage again and answer the following questions with what you hear.

1. When do people start work in American offices?

2. What are American employees expected to do when they have done their own work?

3. How popular is flextime system in Western countries?

4. How are employees in America protected on the matter of employment?

5. What is the atmosphere like in many of the American offices?

Speaking ▶▶|

Discussion

☎ **Work in groups. Discuss and compare the everyday office practice in America and in China. You may find some of the following ideas useful.**

- 📁 Working hours
- 📁 Holidays
- 📁 Lunch breaks
- 📁 Work environment
- 📁 Office hierarchy
- 📁 Dressing code
- 📁 Staff appraisal
- 📁 Staff promotion
- 📁 Efficiency of office procedures

America	China

☎ **Work in groups. Study the results of your comparison carefully and say which aspects you would like to see copied into and which you are glad do not exist in your office. State your reasons.**

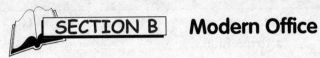

Pre-listening ▶▶

Discussion

· ·

Discuss the following questions with your partner and take notes when necessary.

1. Can you mention some of the office equipment and facilities that are widely used at today's workplace?

----

2. How will the modern office technology change the office work in the future?

Listening ▶▶

Conversation

· ·

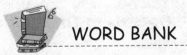

WORD BANK

| instruction | /ɪnˈstrʌkʃən/ | *n.* | 用法说明（书） |

slot	/slɒt/	n.	缝，狭槽
automatically	/ˌɔːtəˈmætɪklɪ/	ad.	自动地
beep	/biːp/	n.	信号音，嘟嘟声

I. Listen to the conversation and decide whether the following statements are true or false. Write T for true and F for false in the brackets.

1. (   ) Both Hans and Jenny work for the Marketing department.

2. (   ) Jenny wants to know how to operate the new fax machine.

3. (   ) Jenny misplaced the fax machine instructions and could not find them any longer.

4. (   ) Jenny wants to send a sales contract to Hans but she does not know how to do it.

5. (   ) The new fax machine is so advanced that it can send two pages at one time.

6. (   ) The fax machine can take in paper automatically so the operator need not feed in paper manually.

7. (   ) When the first page is finished, you will hear a signal, and then you feed in the second page.

8. (   ) When you send all your pages, you have to wait for the line to disconnect and see the display which says: FAX DONE.

II. Listen to the conversation again and write down the steps in operating the fax machine.

Operating Instructions

How to fax a two-page sales contract:

Step 1: (1) _____.

Step 2: (2) _____ and the fax machine takes the page in automatically.

Step 3: (3) _____.

Step 4: (4) _____ and the machine dials the number automatically.

Step 5: Wait for the machine connecting with the fax at the other end and sending the first page automatically.

Step 6: (5) _____ after the first one is finished.

Step 7: (6) _____ and then you see the display there says: FAX DONE.

Passage

WORD BANK

transmit	/trænz'mɪt/	*v.*	传送
eliminate	/ɪ'lɪmɪneɪt/	*v.*	消除
automation	/,ɔ:tə'meɪʃ(ə)n/	*n.*	自动化
showroom	/'ʃəʊrʊm/	*n.*	陈列室
standardize	/'stændədaɪz/	*v.*	使标准化
access	/'ækses/	*v.*	获取(信息)
staple	/'steɪp(ə)l/	*v.*	用订书钉装订
unfounded	/ʌn'faʊndɪd/	*a.*	无理由的
back-up	/'bækʌp/	*n.*	备份

I. Listen to the passage and choose the best answers to the questions you hear.

1. A. In the 1960s and 1970s.   B. In the 1970s and 1980s.
   C. In the 1980s and 1990s.   D. In the 21st century.
2. A. Printer.   B. Computer.
   C. Photocopier.   D. Fax machine.
3. A. Sorting data.   B. Stapling documents.
   C. Issuing standardized letters.   D. Refilling the paper supply bin.
4. A. Purchase orders.   B. Marriage certificates.
   C. Originals of sales agreement.   D. All of the above.
5. A. The widespread use of computers will definitely lead to heavy loss of jobs.
   B. The developments in office technology have led to electronic business (e-business).
   C. New developments in office technology have brought about great changes in the job market.
   D. Automated and electronic practices have eliminated paperwork in modern offices.

II. Listen to the passage again and complete the notes with what you hear.

Modern Office

Developments in office technology:
Machines are employed to do work which (1) _____.
Data is transmitted instantly by way of (2) _____. Much of the (3) _____ has been eliminated.

Impracticability of pure office automation:
Human operators are still needed to (4) _____, (5) _____ _____, (6) _____ and (7) _____ _____ despite the application of computers and advanced office equipment such as the fax machine and the photocopier in modern offices.

Influence of office technology on employment:
New developments in office technology have changed (8) _____

_____, leading to (9) _____ and (10) _____ although some people initially feared that widespread computer use would incur (11) _____.

Automation & office paperwork:

Modern office is unlikely to be paperless. Paper records are still considered desirable for particular documents: as (12) _____ _____; as a means of (13) _____; or as more appropriate in the case of (14) _____ _____, etc. Hard copy — (15) _____ _____ — is still in widespread use in business.

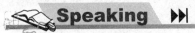 **Speaking** ▶▶|

Discussion

☎ **Work in pairs. Match the following expressions of office facilities with the appropriate Chinese equivalents.**

1. photocopier   a. 电视电话
2. fax machine   b. 台式电脑
3. videophone   c. 激光打印机
4. overhead projector   d. 远程会议系统
5. camcorder   e. 扫描仪
6. shredder   f. 影印机
7. scanner   g. 碎纸机
8. desktop   h. 投影仪
9. laser printer   i. 传真机
10. teleconferencing system   j. 便携式摄录机

☎ **Work in groups. Discuss the following questions with your group members. Take notes when you discuss.**

📁 What are the major uses of the above office equipment in business practices?

📁 What office work would you prefer to do by yourself without help from a machine?

📁 What office work would you be glad to leave a machine to do for you?

📁 If you have the authority and budget to reorganize your office, what office technology would you like to introduce into it?

☎ **Work as a class. Share your insights with the rest of the class.**

Further Listening

Short Recordings

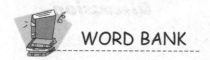

WORD BANK

quarterly	/ˈkwɔːtəlɪ/	*ad.*	每季地
conference	/ˈkɔnfərəns/	*n.*	会议
complimentary	/ˌkɔmplɪˈmentərɪ/	*a.*	（免费）赠送的
deadline	/ˈdedlaɪn/	*n.*	最终期限
urgently	/ˈəːdʒəntlɪ/	*ad.*	迫切地, 急切地
launch	/lɔːntʃ/	*n.*	发行, 投放市场
schedule	/ˈskedʒʊl/	*n.*	时间表, 进度表
optimistic	/ˌɔptɪˈmɪstɪk/	*a.*	乐观的, 有信心的
go ahead			着手，开始
get off			寄出，发出（电报、信件等）

I. In this section, you will hear five short recordings. For each piece, decide what each speaker is trying to do.

Item 1.   ----------------------

Item 2.   ----------------------

Item 3.   ----------------------

Item 4.   ----------------------

Item 5.   ----------------------

A. make an offer

B. confirm an arrangement

C. ask for permission

D. give feedback

E. decline an offer

F. change an arrangement

G. make a complaint

H. request some information

II. Listen to the five recordings again and decide whether the following statements are true or false. Write T for true and F for false in the brackets.

1. (   ) Sue Brock wanted a copy of quarterly sales report of Brenda's department.

2. (   ) Sue called to check some sales figures with Brenda for the quarterly sales report.

3. (   ) Steve Huang rang to inform Brenda when that year's Asian Telecommunications Trade Fair commenced.

4. (   ) Steve Huang was selling trade fair tickets to Brenda and her colleagues.

5. (   ) Colin called to ask if he could put off his next month visit until around the 24th.

6. (   ) Colin would call again to confirm if Brenda was OK with the new arrangement.

7. (   ) John was on a business trip to Hong Kong with a client at the moment.

8. (   ) John asked Brenda to call back on 0853 256 7861 as soon as possible.

9. (   ) Tim responded positively to Brenda's proposal although there was still room for improvement.

10. (   ) Tim was not quite in agreement with Brenda about the time schedule of the product launch.

Home Listening

Business News

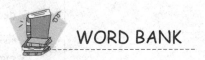 WORD BANK

violate	/ˈvaɪəleɪt/	v.	违反
compromise	/ˈkɒmprəmaɪz/	n.	妥协，和解
honor	/ˈɒnə(r)/	v.	执行，履行，承兑

Listen to the business news report and choose the best answer to complete each of the following sentences.

1. US steel import taxes were initially designed to stay in operation until _____.

   A. March, 2002　　　B. September, 2003　　　C. September, 2004　　　D. March, 2005

2. President Bush ordered the new taxes on imports of steel with a view to _____.

   A. fortifying economic ties with Japan, China and EU countries

   B. obtaining the favor of American voters for the coming election

   C. protecting the domestic steel industry from foreign competition

   D. securing US leading position in the international steel market

3. According to the recent WTO ruling, _____.

   A. EU countries are permitted to tax imports from the United States as punishment

   B. EU countries are permitted to reorganize or purchase American steel companies

   C. US steel import taxes should be sharply lowered during the next four months

   D. US steel import taxes should be removed six months earlier than originally planned

4. If the USA refuses to honor the WTO ruling to cancel steel import taxes, _____.

   A. President Bush might be forced to resign office

   B. exports from the United States are likely to be taxed by other countries

C. American steel-consuming industries will benefit from the price increases

D. American steel companies will suffer a setback for being unable to complete reorganization

5. All of the following can be concluded from the news report EXCEPT that _____.

  A. the steel industry in the United States is at risk when confronted with the competition from other nations

  B. If not handled properly, the US steel tariff dispute might cast shadows upon President Bush's political career

  C. the World Trade Organization is an international system responsible for negotiating trade issues and ruling on trade disputes

  D. President Bush is reluctant to cancel the steel import taxes although officials in his administration object to his decision

Unit 5

• **Business Planning**

Dictation

●●●

Listen to the following short paragraph and fill in the blanks with what you hear.

Business planning is a (1) _____
process. Planning is a dynamic, complex decision-making process where management
evaluates its ability to (2) _____ and to respond to
uncontrollable factors in an environment of uncertainty. Management (3) _____
_____ it believes will be profitable. It
employs (4) _____, especially in accounting,
to (5) _____, make forecasts, construct plans,
(6) _____, make revisions, choose a course of
action, and implement that course of action. After implementation managerial control
consists of efforts to (7) _____,
to record events and their results, and to (8) _____
.

Listening & Speaking

SECTION A   **Planning Your Business**

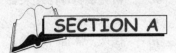

Pre-listening ▶▶

Discussion

● ●

Discuss the following questions with your partner and take notes when necessary.

1. Do you like to make plans for what you are going to do?

....

....

2. How would you prepare for a conference if you are the organizer?

....

....

Listening ▶▶

Conversation

● ●

WORD BANK

pressing	/ˈpresɪŋ/	*a.*	紧迫的

provisionally	/prəˈvɪʒənlɪ/	*ad.*	暂时地, 临时地
seminar	/ˈsemɪnɑː/	*n.*	研究会, 讨论发表会
venue	/ˈvenjuː/	*n.*	会议地点
accommodation	/əˌkɔməˈdeɪʃən/	*n.*	住处, 膳宿

I. Listen to the conversation and choose the best answers to the questions you hear.

1. A. Organizing a weekend party.　　B. Organizing a weekend meeting.
   C. Organizing a weekend lecture.　　D. Organizing a weekend trip.

2. A. Informing some foreign guests of the dates and venue of the conference.
   B. Notifying each speaker when and where they will be giving their speeches.
   C. Instructing each speaker how to get to the hotel from the airport or station.
   D. Preparing the speech papers to facilitate the understanding of the lectures.

3. A. Clarify to each speaker when and where they will be giving their speeches.
   B. Ask the speakers to submit the titles and summaries of their speeches.
   C. Instruct the guests how to get to the hotel from the airport or station.
   D. Make hotel reservations for the guests coming to attend the conference.

4. A. About 50 foreign guests are expected to attend the weekend conference.
   B. All the speakers invited have confirmed their presence at the conference.
   C. The conference is scheduled to last from Friday noon to Sunday evening.
   D. The hotel Annie booked can accommodate up to 70 people at the same time.

5. A. Annie still has got plenty of time to make preparations for the conference.
   B. The conference will attract more foreign guests to come than expected.
   C. The guests invited to the conference are entitled to free accommodations.
   D. Making preparations for a conference is a demanding and exhausting job.

II. Listen to the conversation again and complete the notes with what you hear.

Weekend Conference Memo

Date of conference: (1) _____

Number of delegates: (2) _____

Venue of the conference: (3) _____

Hotel conference facilities:
- 📂 a (4) _____
- 📂 three (5) _____

Conference components:
- 📂 (6) _____ in the main hall
- 📂 (7) _____ in the other rooms

Conference preparations:

What has been done:
— booking provisionally (8) _____

   at the hotel
— sending invitation letters to some foreign guests, telling them (9) _____

   _____, and explaining (10) _____

   _____

What is to be done:
— to send out (11) _____
— to tell each speaker (12) _____
— to give details to each speaker about their accommodations
— to give instructions on (13) _____
— to ask speakers to (14) _____
— to prepare (15) _____

Passage

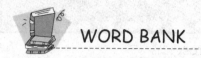

WORD BANK

chaos	/'keɪɔs/	n.	混乱
prioritize	/praɪ'ɔrɪtaɪz/	v.	把……区分优先次序
vital	/'vaɪtl/	a.	重大的，至关重要的
chart	/tʃɑ:t/	v.	制图；制定
critical	/'krɪtɪkəl/	a.	重要的
sidetrack	/'saɪdtræk/	v.	转移目标；使受牵制
reflect	/rɪ'flekt/	v.	反省，细想
drain	/dreɪn/	n.	损耗，消耗

I. Listen to the passage and decide whether the following statements are true or false. Write T for true and F for false in the brackets.

1. (　　) With poor work habits, you will have no chance to survive in business no matter you are an employee or an employer.

2. (　　) Focus on your goals and your sense of focus is essential to your survival and success.

3. (　　) For many new businesses, the priority may be how to stop the cash drain and grow the business to profits.

4. (　　) Owners of new businesses are advised to spend more time generating profits and less time in business planning.

5. (　　) Preparing a priority list improves your efficiency and enables you to accomplish more in less time.

6. (　　) When you feel the pressure of having too much to do, back away, take a few deep breaths and have a rest.

7. (　　) It can be inferred from the passage that the "non-essential tasks" are those that may take one away from his goals.

8. (　　) The passage mainly tells us how business owners can get relieved from heavy workload.

II. Listen to the passage again and complete the following notes with what you hear.

Prioritize Your Workload to Success!

Poorly-organized business people are those who:

📂 manage with (1) _____.

📂 waste their time on (2) _____.

📂 have difficulty in (3)_____.

Responsibilities of a business owner include:

📂 to (4) _____.

📂 to (5) _____.

📂 to (6) _____.

📂 to (7) _____.

To accomplish more in business, you must:

📂 (8) _____.

📂 spend some of your time in (9) _____.

📂 establish (10) _____

and (11) _____.

Preparing a priority list is important in that:

(12) _____.

Speaking ▶▶|

Discussion

☎ **Work in groups. Propose an objective you aim to achieve either in your study, work** or life. Discuss and work out the details of your study, work or life plan. You may structure your discussion on the following steps.

- ❑ Specify your objective
- ❑ Analyze your current status
- ❑ Review resources you may employ
- ❑ Propose approaches to your goal
- ❑ Determine priorities
- ❑ Set schedules

☎ **Work as a class. Present your plan to the rest of the class for further comments or suggestions.**

SECTION B   Creating Business Plans

Pre-listening ▶▶

Discussion

Discuss the following questions with your partner and take notes when necessary.

1. Do you think it essential to develop a business plan before starting a new venture?

----

2. What contents do you expect to find in a business plan?

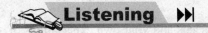

Listening ▶▶|

Conversation

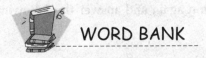

WORD BANK

coach	/kəutʃ/	*v.*	训练，指导
commitment	/kəˈmɪtmənt/	*n.*	许诺，承担的义务
motivated	/ˈməutɪveɪtɪd/	*a.*	有动机的，由······推动的
integrity	/ɪnˈtegrɪtɪ/	*n.*	正直，诚实
clarity	/ˈklærɪtɪ/	*n.*	清楚，透明
accountable	/əˈkauntəbl/	*a.*	应负责的，有责任的
accountability	/əˌkauntəˈbɪlɪtɪ/	*n.*	责任
address	/əˈdres/	*v.*	处理

I. Listen to the conversation and choose the best answers to the questions you hear.

1. A. A consultant.　　　　　　　　　B. An executive.

   C. A coach.　　　　　　　　　　　　D. An accountant.

2. A. By weekly coaching calls.　　　　B. By face-to-face negotiation.

   C. By providing training sessions.　　D. By hiring private investigators.

3. A. Design your business around your clients' needs.

   B. Be motivated, professional and responsible.

   C. Success = Vision + Focus + Clarity + Belief

   D. Everyone has the power to create what he wants.

4. A. The goal should be realistic.

   B. The goal should be in agreement with what the clients want for themselves.

   C. The goal should be in agreement with what is expected from their industry.

   D. The goal should be in agreement with the overall plan.

5. A. A business should center on the clients' needs only.

B. A business should be designed around the clients' needs and your own expectations of life.

C. A business is a way to earn a living.

D. A business has nothing to do with one's life style.

II. Listen to the conversation again and answer the following questions with what you hear.

1. What service does Mr. Alger's company provide?

_____

2. What is a typical business coaching client of Mr. Alger's like?

_____
_____

3. What is the formula for success from Mr. Alger's perspective?

_____

4. What steps will be taken in the goal-setting process?

_____

5. What is the biggest mistake people make when trying to set business goals?

_____

6. What are the "golden rules" about business planning?

_____
_____

Passage

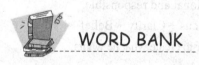

WORD BANK

strategic	/strəˈtiːdʒɪk/	*a.*	战略的, 战略上的

draft	/drɑːft/	*n.*	草稿,草案,草图
random	/'rændəm/	*a.*	任意的,随便的
statistics	/stə'tɪstɪks/	*n.*	统计数字
documentation	/,dɔkjumen'teɪʃən/	*n.*	文件

I. Listen to the passage and choose the best answers to the questions you hear.

1. A. Raise money.
   B. Take on a strategic partner.
   C. Clarify a business plan.
   D. Check the related documentation.

2. A. Visit the local library to get related books.
   B. Access Internet business sites.
   C. Check software packages on business plan.
   D. Buy related books in a book store.

3. A. Check with family members and professionals immediately.
   B. Check the related documentation immediately.
   C. Note the missing information for later consideration.
   D. Rearrange the structure of the plan.

4. A. When he finishes and revises the first draft of the plan.
   B. When he finishes the second version of the plan.
   C. When he finishes the final copy of the plan.
   D. When he checks with other professionals.

5. A. To have a good idea of how the business works.
   B. To have a better handle on the financials.
   C. To have a greater chance to take on a strategic partner.
   D. To complete tasks easily.

6. A. Preparing a business plan is necessary and worthwhile.
   B. Preparing a business plan is an interesting job.
   C. Preparing a business plan is time-consuming.
   D. Preparing a business plan is a gradual process.

II. Listen to the passage again and complete the notes with what you hear.

Steps to Prepare a Business Plan

📁 Clarify what you want to do, for example:
— whether to (1) _____;
— or to (2) _____.

📁 Write (3) _____.

📁 Learn (4) _____ by means of:
— visiting your local library to get a few books with sample business plans;
— accessing (5) _____;
— making use of (6) _____.

📁 Prepare an outline.

📁 Gather all the essential information, such as:
— (7) _____;
— competitive information;
— prepared marketing pieces;
— (8) _____;
— (9) _____.

📁 Put the gathered information into your outline where it fits. You can put down:
— (10) _____ without worrying about grammar;
— ideas that need to be developed;
— (11) _____;
— suggestions collected from other people.

📁 (12) _____ and check your spelling and grammar.

📁 Read your plan, revise it, and (13) _____.

📁 Check with (14) _____, and take their suggestions.

📁 Get the documentation needed to (15) _____.

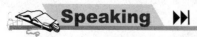 **Speaking** ▶▶

Discussion & Case Study

☎ **Work in groups. Discuss the following case and work out a business plan for the Department. Your business plan should comprise key strategies in the areas of medical practice (e.g. dental treatment to patients in the other communities), service (e.g. routine dental care), and education (e.g. preventive measures), identify clear goals and ensure that the goals are reasonable and achievable.**

Case Study

The Department of Dentistry at the University of Alberta has been merged with an independent dental clinic. But since then it has been troubled by deficit in the operating fund. They want to maintain the quality of teaching, research and medical service. They want to make more investments to ensure competitiveness. They also want to repay the debt owed to the university. But they do not have adequate revenue. Their main problems are how to balance income with expenditure, how to find channels to make money, and how to secure more funding.

☎ **Work as a class. Present your business plan to the rest of the class for their comments or suggestions.**

Further Listening

Short Recordings

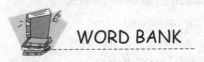
WORD BANK

| tackle | /ˈtæk(ə)l/ | v. | 处理，解决 |
| ingredient | /ɪnˈgriːdɪənt/ | n. | 配料 |

I. In this section, you will hear five short recordings. For each piece, decide what problem each speaker is talking about.

Item 1. ------------------

Item 2. ------------------

Item 3. ------------------

Item 4. ------------------

Item 5. ------------------

A. poor sales figures

B. inexperienced staff

C. poor management

D. staff time-keeping

E. falling share prices

F. retirement of CEO

G. unsatisfactory supplies

H. salary increases

II. Listen to the five recordings again and choose the best answers to the questions you hear.

1. A. Providing them with more training.

   B. Recruiting more hard working people.

   C. Replacing them with more skilled workers.

   D. Rearranging the work shift.

2. A. The CEO should have retired earlier as he has been in the job for six years.

   B. The CEO is difficult to be replaced as he has done such an excellent job.

   C. The CEO has no choice but to go as the competition for the position is intense.

   D. The CEO is eager to leave as he has received a more attractive offer from another company.

3. A. The global economic recession.

   B. The company' poor sales figures.

   C. The company's switchover to new suppliers.

   D. People's lack of enthusiasm for stock investment.

4. A. The issue calls for their immediate action.

   B. Bad management is responsible for the issue.

   C. The issue concerns the product reliability.

   D. The suppliers are blamable for the issue.

5. A. Low salaries.　　　　　　　　　　B. Heavy workload.

   C. Evident sex discrimination.　　　　D. Unfavorable shift arrangements.

Home Listening

Business News

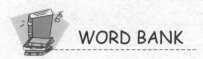

WORD BANK

New York Stock Exchange	纽约证券交易所
Depositary Receipts	存托凭证（在一国证券市场上发行并流通的代表外国发行公司有价证券的可转让凭证）

Listen to the business news report and complete the following notes with what you hear.

New York Stock Exchange

History of New York Stock Exchange (NYSE):
► year of establishment: _____
► year of becoming a non-profit organization: _____

Current business scale of the NYSE:
► number of companies trading on the NYSE: _____
► value of all the stocks trading on the NYSE: _____
► number of foreign companies represented on the NYSE: _____

Types of financial products traded on the NYSE: _____

Membership of the NYSE:

▶ total member number: _____

▶ members' rights: _____

▶ cost of membership: _____

Makeup of the governing board:

▶ 12 _____

▶ 12 _____

▶ 1 _____

▶ 2 _____

Chairman of the NYSE:

▶ the former chairman Richard Grasso resigned in September after the revelation that

_____

_____

▶ the temporary chairman John Reed plans to _____

Unit 6

Management

Dictation

....

Listen to the following short paragraph and fill in the blanks with what you hear.

Some would (1) _____, while others would define it as a science. Whether (2) _____ isn't what is most important. Management is a process that is used to (3) _____; that is, a process that is used to achieve what an organization wants to achieve. An organization could be a business, a school, a city, (4) _____, or (5) _____. Managers are the people to whom (6) _____, and it is generally thought that they achieve the desired goals through the key functions of (7) _____. Some would (8) _____, but for the purposes of this discussion, leading is included as a part of directing.

Listening & Speaking

SECTION A   **Management Functions**

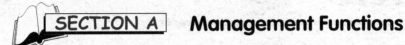

Pre-listening ▶▶

Discussion

● ●

Discuss the following questions with your partner and take notes when necessary.

1. What functions do you think management performs?

----

2. What is a manager's routine work?

Listening ▶▶

Conversation

● ●

WORD BANK

rate	/reɪt/		*n.* 价格

prestige	/preˈstiːʒ/	*n.*	声望, 威望
motivate	/ˈməʊtɪveɪt/	*v.*	使具有……的动机
be stuck with			不得不接纳

I. Listen to the conversation and choose the best answers to the questions you hear.

1. A. Managing Director.

   B. Personnel Director.

   C. Production Director.

   D. Financial Director.

2. A. The company is paying moderate rates to its employees.

   B. The company is paying the best rates to its employees.

   C. The company is paying the worst rates to its employees.

   D. The company is paying competitive rates to its employees.

3. A. An increased production.

   B. An improved quality.

   C. An enhanced corporate reputation.

   D. A decreased staff turnover.

4. A. The company is recognized as the best employer in the industry.

   B. The company is suffering from brain drain caused by underpayment.

   C. The Managing Director wants to be paid with the best rate in the industry.

   D. The Managing Director believes paying competitive wages does not meaning overpaying.

5. A. The management opts for productivity payments instead of overpayment to boost company's competitiveness.

   B. The management hold different perspectives about the impact of pay policy on company reputation.

   C. The Managing Director's proposal to offer the best rates in the industry meets with the management's approval.

   D. The Managing Director is concerned with the increased labor cost resulting from offering competitive wages.

II. Listen to the conversation again and complete the notes with what you hear.

We Offer the Best Rates of Pay!

Plus & minus of offering high pay rates:

From the Managing Director's point of view:

🖉 Giving the company (1) _____

🖉 Helping to (2) _____

🖉 Stopping the company from (3) _____

From the personnel recruitment's point of view:

🖉 Allowing the company to get the right number of people with (4) _____ _____ and (5) _____

🖉 Not ensuring a reputation for (6) _____

Plus & minus of offering productivity payments:

🖉 Encouraging workers to (7) _____

🖉 Not guaranteeing enhanced competitiveness of the company

Risks of offering overpayment:

🖉 Stopping people from moving on and encouraging people to (8) _____ _____

The best option to make:

🖉 Trying to strike a balance — (9) _____ and to get the right people, but not (10) _____

Passage

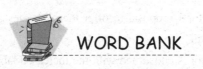

WORD BANK

| feasibility | /ˌfiːzəˈbɪlətɪ/ | *n.* | 可行性 |

allocate	/'æləkeɪt/	*v.*	分配，配给
supervise	/'sjuːpəvaɪz/	*v.*	监督，管理
deviation	/ˌdiːvɪ'eɪʃən/	*n.*	偏向，偏差
corrective	/kə'rektɪv/	*a.*	改正的，纠正的
interactive	/ˌɪntər'æktɪv/	*a.*	相互作用的
simultaneously	/ˌsɪməl'teɪnɪəslɪ/	*ad.*	同时

I. Listen to the passage and decide whether the following statements are true or false. Write T for true and F for false in the brackets.

1. (   ) Managers must select objectives and develop programs which are practicable and acceptable to the employees.

2. (   ) Top management is responsible for making both long-term and short-term business plans.

3. (   ) Organizing teams of IT professionals entails more sophisticated management techniques than organizing assembly-line workers.

4. (   ) Assembly-line proves to be an efficient way to organize the production of a standard product like blue jeans.

5. (   ) Managers are performing the function of organizing when they supervise and guide the employees to do their best.

6. (   ) The activity of leading is more concrete than activities of planning and organizing as it involves working with people.

7. (   ) Through the controlling function, the manager keeps the organization from deviating from its target.

8. (   ) Management involves four major activities, which should be carried out step by step to optimize the management process.

II. Listen to the passage again and complete the notes with what you hear.

Management Basics

Definition of Management:

📁 The process of planning, organizing, leading and controlling (1) _____

_____ .

Major Management Activities:

📁 Planning — the process of (2) _____

_____ .

📁 Organizing — the process of (3) _____

_____ .

📁 Leading — the process of (4) _____

_____ .

📁 Controlling — the process of (5) _____

_____ .

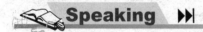

Speaking ▶▶

Discussion & Case study

☎ **Work in groups. Study the following case and discuss the following questions.**

— Where did it go wrong with the management of the organization?

— What method of intervention would you employ at each stage of the decline?

Case Study

An organization has been losing its best staff members. The individuals who departed cited higher pay as the primary reason that they chose to take a new job.

In order to raise the level of pay, managers exhort staff to take on more work. That is, they admit more clients or accept more assignments without a corresponding increase in the number of staff. Thus, income rises. This increased funding is targeted to higher salaries, but the raises cannot be implemented until the next fiscal year (or, the amount of increases actually available for salaries is smaller than hoped after other increases are considered).

Soon, staff are overheard to complain about the workload. Absences from work due to illness increase. The remaining staff members assume even more work. Before long, customers are complaining about poor service which they attribute to insufficient staffing. Most often, these complaints and anger are directed to management because it is apparent that the front line staff have little control over the situation. The result is a decrease in demand for the organization's products.

☎ **Work as a class. Share your insights with your classmates and decide which group's method is most recommendable and why.**

SECTION B Management Styles

Pre-listening ▶▶|

Discussion

Discuss the following questions with your partner and take notes when necessary.

1. What is your impression of Chinese managers' management style?

2. What skills and abilities are desired for management work?

Listing ▶▶▶

Conversation

WORD BANK

foreman	/ˈfɔːmən/	*n.*	(车间的)工长，领班
shift	/ʃɪft/	*n.*	轮班
transformation	/ˌtrænsfəˈmeɪʃ(ə)n/	*n.*	改革，转换
economize	/ɪ(ː)ˈkɒnəmaɪz/	*v.*	节约
utilization	/ˌjuːtɪlaɪˈzeɪʃən/	*n.*	利用，应用
correlate	/ˈkɒrəleɪt/	*v.*	和……相关
bonus	/ˈbəʊnəs/	*n.*	奖金，红利
offset press			胶印机

I. Listen to the conversation and decide whether the following statements are true or false. Write T for true and F for false in the brackets.

1. (   ) Workers at Mr. Chen's workshop usually work on regular shifts, but this week they have to work on three shifts to meet a deadline.

2. (   ) Workers will receive a higher rate for overtime pay if they have to work on

holidays.

3. (　　) Working overtime is not very frequent at Mr. Chen's workshop.

4. (　　) The home-made four-color offset press used at Mr. Chen's workshop is efficient, space-saving and multi-functional.

5. (　　) With the introduction of advanced technology and sophisticated equipment, workshop jobs would become more demanding and stressful.

6. (　　) The production procedures at the workshop used to be manual-based and labor-intensive, but now have been completely mechanized and automated.

7. (　　) A worker's wage depends on his skill level and his years of service at the factory.

8. (　　) Mr. Chen, the foreman of the workshop, is 50 years old this year.

9. (　　) In China men workers usually retire at the age of 60 and women at 55.

10. (　　) Mrs. Simon seems to be very concerned with the worker's pay package and technology level of the workshop.

II. Listen to the conversation again and complete the notes with what you hear.

Welcome to our workshop

Major technological advances at the workshop:
- (1) _____
- (2) _____

Focus of technical transformation:
- To (3) _____
- To (4) _____
- To (5) _____

Staff advancement efforts:
- Workers are encouraged to (6) _____
  _____, for instance, (7) _____
  _____, or attending TV Classes.

Employee pay policy:

📁 Wages are determined by (8) _____

_____.

📁 Wages comprise (9) _____

_____

Retirement plan:

📁 Retired workers will get a pension to cover their daily necessities.

📁 Skilled workers will be (10) _____,

with a total income higher than before they retired.

Passage

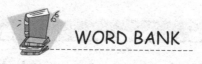

WORD BANK

horde	/hɔːd/	*n.*	一大群，一伙
insular	/ˈɪnsjʊlə/	*a.*	褊狭的
spice	/spaɪs/	*v.*	增加趣味
anecdote	/ˈænɪkdəʊt/	*n.*	逸闻，趣事
terrain	/ˈtereɪn/	*n.*	地势，地形
sloppy	/ˈslɒpɪ/	*a.*	懒散拖沓的
concession	/kənˈseʃən/	*n.*	让步
improvise	/ˈɪmprəvaɪz/	*v.*	临时准备
the old boy network			老同学关系网
go by the book			照章办事

I. Listen to the passage and choose the best answers to the questions you hear.

1. A. American managers.   B. British managers.
   C. German managers.   D. Japanese managers.
2. A. American managers.   B. British managers.
   C. German managers.   D. Japanese managers.
3. A. American managers.   B. British managers.
   C. German managers.   D. Japanese managers.
4. A. They are cunning.   B. They are self-restrained.
   C. They are shrewd.   D. They are aggressive.
5. A. American managers tend to blame their failure upon unfair competition mechanism.
   B. Japanese managers are noted for their sense of hierarchy and seniority.
   C. German managers value education background more than work experience.
   D. British managers have the best knowledge of their company's operations.

II. Listen to the passage again and complete the notes with what you hear.

Telephone Etiquette Checklist

Professional qualifications:

▶ American managers: (1) _____
   _____

▶ British managers: (2) _____
   _____

▶ German managers: (3) _____
▶ Japanese managers: (4) _____

At the business meetings:

▶ American managers: (5) _____
   _____

▶ British managers: (6) _____
   _____

▶ German managers: (7) _____
▶ Japanese managers: (8) _____

Talking manners:

▶ American managers: (9) _____

▶ British managers: (10) _____

▶ German managers: (11) _____

_____

▶ Japanese managers: (12) _____

Speaking ▶▶|

Discussion

☎ Work in groups. List five to six important managerial positions in a company and discuss what skills and abilities are desirable for these positions.

Managerial Positions	Skills & Abilities
Marketing manager	

☎ Work in groups. Suppose you are charged to recruit management staff for a start-up company. Discuss and decide:

— Who do you think is the best candidate in your class for each of the positions listed above?

— What do you think makes him or her the best candidate for the position?

☎ **Work as a class. Announce and explain your appointment decisions to the rest of the class.**

Further Listening

Short Recordings

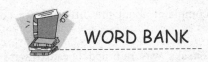

WORD BANK

apparently	/əˈpærəntlɪ/	*ad.*	显然地
warehouse	/ˈweəhaʊs/	*n.*	仓库, 货栈
slab	/slæb/	*n.*	厚平板
acknowledge	/əkˈnɒlɪdʒ/	*v.*	承认
covering letter			附信

I. In this section, you will hear five short recordings. For each piece, decide what the main reason for the message is.

Item 1.　............................

Item 2.　............................

Item 3.　............................

Item 4.　............................

Item 5.　............................

A. making an apology

B. offering to help

C. asking for information

D. amending an order

E. giving instructions

F. canceling an appointment

G. making a complaint

H. explaining a procedure

II. Listen to the five recordings again and decide whether the following statements are true or false. Write T for true and F for false in the brackets.

1. (   ) Matthew can't go for the meeting tomorrow at eleven as he will have a big order to negotiate on behalf of his boss.

2. (   ) Matthew has to stay at the warehouse to take charge of everything as his boss doesn't trust the staff there to handle the order by themselves.

3. (   ) To prepare for the arrival of the inspectors, Mandy left the presentation early and cancelled her meeting with the boss.

4. (   ) Mandy had to leave the presentation early as she had to answer an urgent phone call from her boss.

5. (   ) Frank calculated the area incorrectly and he wanted to change his order to 24 paving slabs in total.

6. (   ) Frank made a complaint about the difference in color of the paving slabs he ordered.

7. (   ) One of Rob's checks was returned because there was allegedly no enough money in his account to cover it.

8. (   ) The company has cancelled the car Rob ordered because Judy Smith had called to say Rob's credit was poor.

9. (   ) Under the company complaints system, customers will receive a copy of the complaints procedure and an apologizing letter.

10. (   ) Customers will not be contacted until all the facts about the situation have been made clear.

Home Listening

Business News

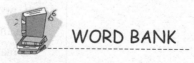

WORD BANK

incur	/ɪnˈkɜː(r)/	v.	招致

constitute	/ˈkɒnstɪtjuːt/	*v.*	构成，组成
reversal	/rɪˈvɜːs(ə)l/	*n.*	逆转
contemplate	/ˈkɒntempleɪt/	*v.*	沉思，考虑
deem	/diːm/	*v.*	认为
consecutive	/kənˈsekjʊtɪv/	*a.*	连续的
seasoned	/ˈsiːznd/	*a.*	有经验的
American Association of Retired Persons			美国退休人员协会

Listen to the business news report and choose the best answers to the questions you hear

1. A. About 500.　　　B. About 700.　　　C. About 1000.　　　D. About 1500.

2. A. Devotion to their career.　　　　B. Desire to remain active.

　C. Losses in the stock market.　　　D. Changing expectations for retirement

3. A. The US stock market in the late 1990s saw a rapid growth.

　B. The US stock market in the late 1990s suffered serious downturns.

　C. The US stock market in the late 1990s underwent great transformation.

　D. The US stock market in the late 1990s experienced ups and downs in turn.

4. A. They lost their jobs in consequence of adverse market conditions.

　B. They were tired of dull wok and wished to enjoy golden retirement years early.

　C. They could receive enough retirement pensions to carry them through "golden years".

　D. They earned enough from the booming stock market to maintain a decent life after retirement.

5. A. Older workers are more active.

　B. Older workers are more experienced.

　C. Older workers are less concerned with pay.

　D. Older workers are more devoted to their profession.

Unit 7

Successful Businesses

Dictation

....

Listen to the following short paragraph and fill in the blanks with what you hear.

To ensure the success of your business, always remember your business is more than just the (1) _____. Recognize that you need to be committed to the whole experience of conducting business to (2) _____ _____, fixing problems, and providing solutions. (3) _____ _____ start out only to make money. But the most successful businesses strive to be greater than their competitors by (4) _____ _____. Before you decide (5) _____ _____ you want to provide, find out more about your customers. Create a strategy to consistently (6) _____ and you will have customers for life. The commitment must be (7) _____ and (8) _____.

Listening & Speaking

Successful Entrepreneurs

Pre-listening ▶▶|

Discussion

Discuss the following questions with your partner and take notes when necessary.

1. What drives people to become entrepreneurs?

----

2. How do you like the life of a successful entrepreneur?
   ❑ Do you dream of becoming a successful entrepreneur?
   ❑ Do you want to marry a successful entrepreneur?
   ❑ Do you want to work for a successful entrepreneur?

Listening ▶▶|

Conversation

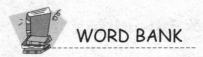

WORD BANK

intrigue	/ɪnˈtriːg/	v.	激起……的兴趣
flair	/fleə(r)/	n.	才能，本领
criteria	/kraɪˈtɪərɪə/	n.	标准
overhead	/ˈəʊvəhed/	n.	管理费
invoicing	/ˈɪnvɔɪsɪŋ/	n.	开发票；托运
burn out			耗尽
throw in the towel			认输
catch up			吸引，迷住

I. Listen to the conversation and decide whether the following statements are true or false. Write T for true and F for false in the brackets.

1. (   ) Kathy started her own business when her children reached school age.

2. (   ) Kathy once worked as an engineer, which she had to drop after marriage.

3. (   ) Kathy used to be a working mother and now she is the owner of a home based business.

4. (   ) Kathy was drawn to the gift basket business because she did her research and found out it was a very lucrative business.

5. (   ) Kathy started her business on impulse and thus had a hard time in the early years of her business.

6. (   ) Kathy is determined to build a successful gift basket company and she has never thought of giving up.

7. (   ) Low overhead is one of the advantages of running a gift basket business from the home.

8. (   ) Without a website, it would have been very difficult and certainly more expensive for Kathy to service and reach customers both domestic and overseas.

II. Listen to the conversation again and answer the questions with what you hear.

1. Why did Kathy decide to start her home-based business?

_____

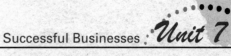
2. What makes the gift basket business right for Kathy?

_____

_____

3. What does Kathy enjoy especially about running her business from the home?

_____

_____

4. How does Kathy market her gift basket business?

_____

5. Apart from designing, what else does a gift basket business owner need to take care of?

_____

_____

Passage

• •

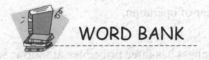

WORD BANK

sustainable	/sə'steɪnəbl/	*a.*	足可支撑的，可持续的
revenue	/'revɪnjuː/	*n.*	收入
deadbeat	/'dedbiːt/	*n.*	<俗> 赖债不还的人
milestone	/'maɪlstəun/	*n.*	里程碑，转折点
alleviate	/ə'liːvɪeɪt/	*v.*	减轻
Ivy League			（美国东北部哈佛、哥伦比亚等八所名牌大学的）常春藤联合会，属于该联合会的名牌大学

I. Listen to the passage and choose the best answers to the questions you hear.

1. A. Get as much funding as possible from investors.
   B. Sell its products and services to customers.

C. Establish its brand among customers.

D. Enjoy the fruits of one's labor.

2. A. Get on the phone and make a collection call.

B. Send letters to remind your customer about the payment.

C. Collect payments when goods and services are delivered.

D. Offer customers a discount for early payments.

3. A. Assign your staff to do the job for you.

B. Turn the task to a commercial collection company.

C. Ask for partial payment.

D. Both A and B.

4. A. Set up a small monthly salary for yourself.

B. Reinvest in your business in order for it to grow.

C. Use the money your business generates on the staff.

D. Buy insurance for yourself and your staff.

5. A. At the very beginning of operation.

B. Six months later.

C. At the end of first year of operation.

D. Two years later.

6. A. Every successful business has three principles to follow: sell, collect and profit.

B. A business can only sustain if it has steady revenue resulting from sales from its customers.

C. A successful entrepreneur must be very busy to keep the business growing.

D. You need to save the capital to sustain your business through the first six months of operation.

II. Listen to the passage again and decide which of the following statements is true. Put a tick (√) for your choice in the brackets.

1. (   ) To be a successful entrepreneur, you need a graduate degree in business from an Ivy League school.

2. (   ) A business can only be sustainable if its lifeline is tied up to the pockets of investors.

3. (   ) You need to know the reason why the customer is late with the payment in order to know the best course of action to take.

4. (   ) The key to collecting money from customers is to bill your customers without

delay.

5. (　) You must not count on spending the money coming in from your business during the first six months of operation.

6. (　) The first six months of operation for a business is critical.

7. (　) Eventually, you'll have other people doing part of the work for you.

8. (　) Starting your own business means a more stable employment than working for others.

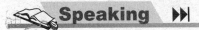 **Speaking** ▶▶▎

Quiz & Discussion

☎ Work alone. Work through the quiz by yourself and see whether you have got the potential to be a successful entrepreneur. Be as honest as you can. Your teacher will interpret what your quiz results mean.

QUIZ

When it comes to developing relationships with new people:

a) I enjoy it, meeting new people energizes me.

b) I do when I have to, but I find meeting new people intimidating.

When I make decisions:

a) Making decisions comes easily to me.

b) I find it hard to reach decisions — often all the alternatives look equally good.

When I make decisions:

a) I always consider how my decisions will affect the bottom line.

b) I think more about how my decision will affect those involved.

My talent lies in:

a) Analyzing the current situation.

b) Looking at the possibilities.

When it comes to selling my products, my ideas and myself:

a) I enjoy the challenge.

b) I feel uncomfortable with the whole process.

What really gets my juices going is:

a) Planning and completing a project.

b) Conceiving the idea for a project.

When it comes to day-to-day administrative duties:

a) I am detail-oriented and organized.

b) I have trouble staying focused.

I feel most comfortable:

a) After I make a decision, I like to know that things are settled.

b) Before I make a decision, I prefer to stay open to possibilities.

When things don't go as planned:

a) I get thrown off-balance.

b) I go with the flow.

I prefer a work environment that is:

a) Lively, where I am able to interact with others throughout the day.

b) Quiet, where I am able to focus on my work.

When I think about writing a business plan:

a) I start planning how and where to begin.

b) I shudder.

☎ **Work in groups. Discuss what contributes most to the success of an entrepreneur. The following points are for your reference.**

— Does a successful entrepreneur usually receive better education than average people?

— Does a successful entrepreneur enjoy being competitive with others?

— Does being successful have more to do with good luck and knowing the right people than with skill and hard work?

— What kinds of people are more likely to rise to the top in the business world?

— In what fields are young entrepreneurs more likely to make a fortune?

☎ **Work in pairs. Go through the Entrepreneurial Qualifications list with your partner and tell each other what qualities you have or do not have as a successful entrepreneur. Illustrate your points.**

Entrepreneurial Qualifications

The following are some of the qualities of successful entrepreneurs. Check and see whether you have these qualities too.

1. Do you like to take charge and make your own decisions?
2. Do you enjoy being competitive with others?
3. Are you a self-directed person with strong self-discipline?
4. Do you plan ahead and consistently meet your goals and objectives?
5. Are you good at time management and getting things done in a punctual manner?
6. Would you be willing to lower your standard of living in order to get a business started?
7. Do you persevere regardless of setbacks?
8. Do you take responsibility for mistakes?
9. Do you listen objectively to advice and criticism given by others?
10. Are you a self-starter?

☎ **Work in groups. Tell your group members how you see your partner's chance of being successful in business, judging from what you've learned about your partner in the previous pair work activity.**

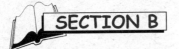

SECTION B **Successful Businesses**

Pre-listening ▶▶|

Discussion

Discuss the following questions with your partner and take notes when necessary.

1. Can you name some successful businesses, both home and abroad, and tell what mainly contributes to their success?

Company	Industry	Major competitors	Secret to success

2. What do you think are important factors leading to a successful business?

 **Listening** ▶▶

Conversation

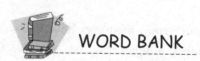 WORD BANK

initially	/ɪˈnɪʃəlɪ/	*ad.*	最初，开头
assemble	/əˈsembl/	*v.*	装配
infancy	/ˈɪnfənsɪ/	*n.*	开始，初期
portion	/ˈpɔːʃən/	*n.*	一部分，一份
affiliate	/əˈfɪlɪeɪt/	*n.*	分支机构
reside	/rɪˈzaɪd/	*v.*	居住
joint-venture company			合资公司

I. Listen to the conversation and decide whether the following statements are true or false. Write T for true and F for false in the brackets.

1. (   ) The company was first established in 1983 and transformed into a joint-venture company in 1986.

2. (   ) The company was the first Chinese company which established business relationship with western partners.

3. (   ) The company manufactured television sets at its early stage.

4. (   ) The founder of the company was introduced to computer technology when he was studying overseas.

5. (   ) The company assembled a variety of computer systems developed by its American partners.

6. (   ) It was a critical decision to make for an enterprise to enter the computer manufacturing field in the mid 1980's.

7. (   ) The company has ranked as one of the leading manufacturers of both computer software and hardware in China.

8. (   ) More than 60% of the enterprises in China are using products manufactured by the company.

9. (   ) The company puts its advertisements in newspapers, popular magazines and trade journals.

10. (   ) The company spends most of its advertising budget on TV commercials as they prove to be most effective.

II. Listen to the conversation again and complete the notes with what you hear.

Do You Know Our Company?

Company Profile
□ time of establishment: (1) _____
□ initial products: (2) _____
□ current product: (3) _____

☐ source of technological assistance: (4) _____

☐ location of headquarters: (5) _____

Market Distribution

☐ exporting (6) _____

☐ with the biggest market in (7) _____

☐ with a rapidly growing (8) _____ market

☐ more than (9) _____ using its products

Company Size

☐ (10) employing _____ people in total

☐ (11) _____ traveling all around the world

☐ about 1,000 employees (12) _____

Passage

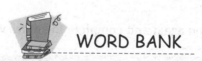

WORD BANK

synonymous	/sɪˈnɒnɪməs/	a.	同义的
dynamo	/ˈdaɪnəməʊ/	n.	发电机
cornerstone	/ˈkɔːnəstəʊn/	n.	墙角石；基石，基础
innovative	/ˈɪnəʊveɪtɪv/	a.	创新的，革新的
euro	/ˈjʊərəʊ/	n.	欧元

Siemens AG	西门子公司（AG 为德语 Aktiengesellschaft 的缩略形式，意为"股份有限公司"）
Werner Siemens	西门子公司创始人之一
Johann Georg Halske	西门子公司创始人之一

I. Listen to the passage and complete the table with what you hear.

<table>
<tr><th colspan="3">From Workshop to Global Player</th></tr>
<tr><th>When</th><th>What Events</th><th>By Whom</th></tr>
<tr><td>(1) _____</td><td>(2) _____.</td><td>Werner Siemens & Johann George Halske</td></tr>
<tr><td>(3) _____</td><td>(4) _____.</td><td>Werner Siemens</td></tr>
<tr><td>1966</td><td>(5) _____.</td><td></td></tr>
<tr><td>Fiscal 2002</td><td>(6) _____.</td><td>Siemens in China</td></tr>
</table>

II. Listen to the passage again and complete the notes with what you hear.

Siemens AG

Siemens Worldwide

As one of the largest companies in the world electrical industry, Siemens has:

★ a presence (1) _____.

★ (2) _____ in more than 50 countries.

★ (3) _____ employees in total.

★ (4) _____ employees in China.

Research & Development

As a highly innovative company, Siemens has:

★ (5) _____ per day.

Siemens Business

Business areas cover:

★ (6) _____ .

★ automation and control.

★ (7) _____ .

★ (8) _____ .

★ medical.

★ (9) _____ .

★ (10) _____ .

The most important areas include:

★ (11) _____ .

Corporate Principles

The function of the corporate principles is:

★ to determine (12) _____ .

The contents of the Corporate Principles are as follows:

★ We strengthen our customers to keep them competitive.

★ We (13) _____ .

★ We enhance company value to (14) _____ .

★ We empower our people to (15) _____ .

★ We embrace (16) _____ .

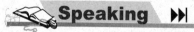 **Speaking** ▶▶

Discussion

☎ **Work alone. Suppose you have just started a small company. In order to run your business successfully, of course you have got a lot of critical decisions to make. Consider the following situations and try to reach a decision in each case.**

☎ **Work in groups. Compare and defend your decisions within your group.**

1. Will you pay higher than average salaries or will you introduce a profit-sharing scheme?

2. Will you send your senior managers to expensive training seminars to improve their performance?

3. Will you spend a large sum of money on long-term research and development projects?

4. Will you hire "mobile employees" (people working at home and staying in touch by phone or computer)?

5. Will you make your staff travel economy class rather than business class to save money?

6. Will you have a company fitness room for the staff to use during breaks and after hours?

7. Will you make a long-term or a short-term plan for your company's growth and development?

8. Will you make most of the decisions or have a team-style management in the company?

9. Will you hire someone for a responsible position who hasn't had a traditional academic education?

10. Will you offer in-service language or computer training for staff during working hours?

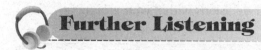
Further Listening

Short Recordings

WORD BANK

emergency	/ɪˈmɜːdʒənsɪ/	n.	紧急情况，突发事件
delegation	/ˌdelɪˈgeɪʃ(ə)n/	n.	代表团
cabinet	/ˈkæbɪnɪt/	n.	（有抽屉或格子的）橱柜
sue	/sjuː/	v.	起诉，控告
chap	/tʃæp/	n.	<口> 家伙，小伙子
consultant	/kənˈsʌltənt/	n.	顾问
short list			供最后挑选用的候选人名单

I. In this section, you will hear five short recordings. For each piece, decide what sort of visitor each speaker is expecting.

Item 1. ----------------------

Item 2. ----------------------

Item 3. ----------------------

Item 4. ----------------------

Item 5. ----------------------

A. Management Consultant

B. Company Solicitor

C. Security Officer

D. Health & Safety Officer

E. Research Officer

F. Human Resources Officer

G. Training Manager

H. Foreign Purchaser

II. Listen to the five recordings again and choose the best answers to the questions you hear.

1. A. How to handle medical emergencies.　　B. How to manage your time better.

　C. How to develop strategic thinking.　　D. How to deal with foreign delegations.

2. A. The staff working regulations.　　B. The health and safety regulations.

　C. The labor insurance regulations.　　D. The equipment operating regulations.

3. A. He is coming to give the staff a presentation.

　B. He is going to visit the Research Department.

　C. He is likely to place a big order with the company.

　D. He is interested in the newly launched product range.

4. A. The urgency of reducing the staff levels.

　B. The legal implications of making staff redundant.

　C. The feasibility of cutting down on the workforce.

　D. The revision of staff employment contracts.

5. A. To be interviewed for the management position.　　B. To discuss the staff recruitment advert.

　C. To interview job applicants.　　D. To make interview arrangements.

Home Listening

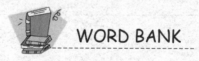

Business News

WORD BANK

speculator	/ˈspekjuleɪtə/	*n.*	投机者
The Chicago Board of Trade			美国芝加哥期货交易所（成立于 1848 年 4 月 3 日,是世界上第一个期货与期权交易所, 它是目前世界上交易规模最大、最具代表性 的农产品交易所）

| Chicago Mercantile Exchange | 美国芝加哥商业交易所（成立于 1898 年，现为美国最大的期货交易所，世界上最大的金融衍生品交易所，世界上第二大买卖期货和期货期权合约的交易所） |
| Commodity Futures Trading Commission | 美国商品期货交易委员会（美国期货市场监管机构之一） |

I. Listen to the business news report and complete the notes with what you hear.

Commodity Contracts:

✓ are agreements to (1) _____

_____ .

✓ represent (2) _____ .

Forward Contracts:

✓ guarantee (3) _____ .

Futures:

✓ are contracts that (4) _____ .

✓ pay the difference (5) _____

_____ .

The Chicago Board of Trade:

✓ In 1848: (6) _____ .

✓ By 1865: (7) _____ .

The Chicago Mercantile Exchange:

✓ Range of products: (8) _____

_____ .

✓ Participants: (9) _____ .

Speculators in the Futures Market:

✓ can cause big changes in the price of futures.

✓ helps provide (10) _____.

Unit 8

Investment

Preliminary Listening

Dictation

Listen to the following short paragraph and fill in the blanks with what you hear.

Investment, the process of exchanging income for an asset that is expected to (1) _____
_____, may be influenced by factors such as rates of interest, the
(2) _____ about future demand and profit,
technical changes in production methods, and expected (3) _____
_____. A portfolio is a collection of investments held by an institution or a private
individual. In building up an investment portfolio a financial institution will typically
(4) _____, whilst a private individual may make use
of the services of a financial advisor or a financial institution which offers (5) _____
_____. The assets in the portfolio could include stocks, bonds,
options, warrants, gold certificates, (6) _____, futures contracts, (7) _____
_____, or any other item that is expected to (8) _____.

Listening & Speaking

SECTION A　Foreign Investment

Pre-listening ▶▶

Discussion

• •

Discuss the following questions with your partner and take notes when necessary.

1. What will you take into consideration if you are to invest in a foreign country?

....

....

2. What is the impact of foreign investment on China's economic development?

....

....

Listening ▶▶

Conversation

• •

WORD BANK

| license | /ˈlaɪsəns/ | *v.* | 批准，特许 |

bilateral	/baɪˈlætərəl/	*a.*	双边的
take	/teik/	*n.*	观点，看法
high-profile	/haɪˈprəʊfaɪl/	*a.*	引人注目的，备受瞩目的；高调的
lease	/liːs/	*v.*	出租，租赁
abide	/əˈbaɪd/	*v.*	坚持，遵守
implementation	/ˌɪmplɪmenˈteɪʃən/	*n.*	执行
capitalize (on)	/ˈkæpɪtəlaɪz/	*v.*	利用
CitiCorp	/ˈsɪtɪkɔːp/		花旗银行
General Electric			通用电气公司
Boeing			波音公司

I. Listen to the conversation and choose the best answers to complete the following statements.

1. According to _____, the US has become the 13th largest foreign investor in Vietnam.

    A. the official statistics

    B. the American Chamber of Commerce in Vietnam

    C. the Vietnam News

    D. Mr. Chris Tragakis

2. Mr. Chris Tragakis _____.

    A. chairs the Vietnam Chamber of Commerce

    B. paves the way for the implementation of the BTA

    C. is credited with having attracted 14 American investment projects

    D. emphasizes the significance of open, competitive and transparent markets to the success of US companies

3. According to Mr. Chris Tragakis, _____ are prospering throughout the full range of Vietnam's economy.

    A. US businesses, regardless of their size   B. only large US corporations

    C. Vietnam-US joint ventures   D. foreign invested businesses

4. The implementation of the BTA will _____.

    A. deteriorate the local business environment

    B. enhance the market competitiveness of Vietnam

    C. improve the quality of life of the local population

D. divert the direction of Vietnamese economic development

5. To compete with its more economically advanced neighbors in drawing US projects, Vietnam is advised to _____.

   A. reduce the tariff rates on the US imports

   B. offer US businesses more preferential policies

   C. build a healthy local business environment

   D. open more areas of economy to foreign investors

II. Listen to the conversation again and complete the notes with what you hear.

Performance and Prospects of American Firms in Vietnam

Areas likely to attract American investors:

❖ _____

❖ _____

❖ _____

❖ _____

❖ _____

Market features American investors would prefer:

❖ _____

❖ _____

❖ _____

Factors that affect the competitiveness of a market:

❖ _____

❖ _____

❖ _____

Areas a country should invest in to build up a healthy local market:

❖ _____

❖ _____

Passage

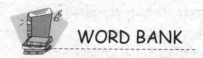

WORD BANK

dividend	/ˈdɪvɪdend/	*n.*	股息，红利

I. Listen to the passage and choose the best answers to the questions you hear.

1. A. The business is not operating well.
   B. The business is suffering from a shortage of capital.
   C. The business needs to raise money for expansion.
   D. The business is looking for business partners.

2. A. $500. B. $600. C. $1,000. D. $1,100.

3. A. $100. B. $200. C. $600. D. $1,000.

4. A. It directly reflects the performance of the company concerned.
   B. It is hard to predict whether the price of a stock will go up or down.
   C. The price of the stock of a profitable company is likely to go up more than others.
   D. The price of a stock goes up only when it is favored by investors in the market.

5. A. Everyone expects to win, but their chance for success is hardly predictable.
   B. Everyone has a chance to win, believe it or not.
   C. In comparison with investment of other kinds, people are more likely to profit from this.
   D. By investing in the stock market, one may be able to make money in the easy way.

II. Listen to the passage again and answer the questions with what you hear.

1. What is dividend?

_____

_____

2. How often do shareholders get their dividends?

_____

3. Besides dividend, what is the other means by which an investor may make money?

_____

4. What is the chief responsibility of a stock broker?

_____

5. What did the stock broker do to help the Smiths to buy the shares?

_____

6. How does the speaker feel about trading stocks as a means of investment?

_____

7. What is usually true of all stocks?

_____

8. What are companies that need money glad about?

_____

Speaking ▶▶

Discussion & Role-play

* *

An important part of the economic reform process in China has been the promotion of foreign direct investment (FDI) inflow. After more than twenty years of economic reform, China has become one of the most important destinations for cross-border direct investment. In recent years, FDI to China accounts for 1/4 to 1/3 of total FDI inflow to developing countries.

How much do you know about China?
CHINA
❑ is the largest mobile phone market in the world.
❑ is the second largest PC market in the world.
❑ has currently over 68m Internet users.
❑ is No. 1 importer of engineering plastics in the world.
❑ produces over 50% of the world's shoes.

☐ will import about US$1.4 trillion worth of equipment and technology from 2002 to 2007.

☐ will build 100 new airports in the next 15 years.

☐ has 630 million people under the age of 25.

☐ has 34 cities with population of over 1 million.

☐ will be the top tourist destination by 2020.

☐ has overtaken US as the most attractive nation for FDI — Nearly 400 of the Fortune 500 have invested in China.

☎ **Work in groups. Read the above statistics carefully and discuss with your group what makes China the most attractive nation for FDI inflow.**

☎ **Work in groups. Discuss the general investment environment in your city or area and decide:**

✓ whether the environment is favorable for foreign investment or not.
✓ what the local government and residents can do to improve the investment environment.

☎ **Work as a class. Suppose you are a spokesman or spokeswoman of the local government and are addressing a group of potential foreign investors. Give them an account of local investment environment, based upon the results of your discussion.**

SECTION B   **Investment Portfolio**

Pre-listening ▶▶

Discussion

Discuss the following questions with your partner and take notes when necessary.

1. What investment options are available for individual investors in the local market?

----

2. What is your favorite investment option and why?

Listening ▶▶|

Conversation

WORD BANK

equity	/ˈekwɪtɪ/	*n.*	资产净值；（*pl*）公司普通股
hand	/hænd/	*n.*	转手，经手
dynamics	/daɪˈnæmɪks/	*n.*	（人或事物）相互作用的方式
gloom	/gluːm/	*n.*	忧愁；萧条
boom	/buːm/	*n.*	繁荣
glamorous	/ˈglæmərəs/	*a.*	富有魅力的，迷人的
slum	/slʌm/	*n.*	贫民窟
charted accountant			<英>（有合格证书的）特许会计师

I. Listen to the conversation and choose the best answers to the questions you hear.

1. A. An expert in property investment. B. A consultant in property investment.
   C. The owner of an investment firm. D. A guest host for a financial program.

2. A. Make investments for future profit.

B. Deposit money in the bank and wait for the rates to rise.

C. Sell the investment one has previously made.

D. Keep the money as nest egg for security's sake.

3. A. Ancient houses in the downtown area.　B. Houses in the slum areas.

C. Average houses for average people.　D. Low-priced houses in the suburbs.

4. A. The time of the purchase.　B. The type of properties purchased.

C. The number of properties purchased.　D. The equity of all the current investment.

5. A. Keep properties for rents for the long-term profit.

B. Buy in gloom and keep the properties for rents.

C. Buy in gloom and sell in boom.

D. Change hands as quickly as possible.

II. Listen to the conversation again and decide whether the following statements are true or false. Write T for true and F for false in the brackets.

1. (　　) Steve invested in real estates because his friends recommended that to him.

2. (　　) At the moment, Steve still has 170 houses in his hand.

3. (　　) Steve started from a relatively small capital.

4. (　　) Steve differed from other investors in the way of handling business.

5. (　　) According to Steve, a positive cash flow means the cash you receive should be equal to the amount that you pay out.

6. (　　) When interest rates go up, houses will be in greater demand in the property market.

7. (　　) In order to make the greatest profit, it is important for the investor to do everything by himself.

8. (　　) We can learn from the interview that property investing is just for the rich and better off.

Passage

WORD BANK

diversified	/daɪˈvəːsɪfaɪd/	*a.*	多变化的，各种的
portfolio	/pɔːtˈfəʊljəʊ/	*a.*	投资组合
roller-coaster	/ˈrəʊləˌkəʊstə/	*n.*	过山车
Leonardo da Vinci			李奥纳多·达·芬奇（意大利的著名美术家、雕塑家、建筑家、工程师和科学家，1452—1519）

I. Listen to the passage and decide whether the following statements are true or false. Write T for true and F for false in the brackets.

1. (   ) It is important for investors to set a clear goal for the near future.

2. (   ) Investments are full of risks which are not always predictable.

3. (   ) The more money one invests, the more money he reaps.

4. (   ) New York stocks have remained strong since the year 1900.

5. (   ) New York stocks have averaged 30% annual returns over the past several years.

6. (   ) The more diversified your investment portfolio is, the less losses you would sustain.

7. (   ) It calls for prudence and patience to profit from investment in the long run.

8. (   ) The passage is presented to help novice investors make sound investment decisions.

II. Listen to the passage again and complete the notes with what you hear.

Guidelines to Smart Investment

The guidelines for smart investing:

✎ (1) _____

✎ (2) _____

✎ (3) _____

Your investment portfolio may include:

✎ (4) _____

✎ (5) _____

✎ (6) _____

✎ (7) _____

✎ (8) _____

Annual returns from stock investment:

✎ Over the past several years, (9) _____

✎ Since the year 1900, (10) _____

Quotations by Leonardo da Vinci:

"(11) _____"

Speaking ▶▶

Discussion & Role-play

Being the Investment Portfolio Consultants, you are required to help clients reach their financial goals and lead your clients from where they are today to where they dream to be. You are also required to provide investment guidance and tailor-made financial solution to individual investors through face-to-face consultations.

☎ **Work in groups. Below is a table that shows the annual returns for four hypothetical portfolios. Suppose you only had these investment options, study the table and decide which of the four you would choose. Announce your investment option to your group and explain your choice.**

	Minimum Annual Total Return Average	Average Annual Total Return	Maximum Annual Total Return
Portfolio A	3%	7%	11%
Portfolio B	−4%	9%	19%
Portfolio C	−9%	11%	27%
Portfolio D	−16%	13%	40%

☎ Work in pairs. Take turns to play the role of an investment portfolio consultant and an individual investor seeking investment guidance. Interview your partner for information concerning his or her family's financial objectives, investment expectations, tolerance for risk, investment time frame, assets and liabilities, income and expenditure, life stage of family members, and etc.

☎ Work in pairs. Tailor a family investment portfolio for your partner. Discuss with your partner and see if your portfolio has the potential to provide the return your partner wants at the level of risk your partner feels comfortable with.

Further Listening

Short Recordings

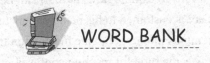

WORD BANK

irritate	/ˈɪrɪteɪt/	v.	引起不愉快，引起恼怒
desperately	/ˈdespərɪtlɪ/	ad.	不顾一切地，拼命地
at an angle			倾斜地，成一定角度
have a go			尝试
PA			私人助理（即 Personal Assistant）

I. In this section, you will hear five short recordings. For each piece, decide which aspect of a colleague each speaker is complaining about.

Item 1. ----------------------------

Item 2. ----------------------------

Item 3. ----------------------------

Item 4. ----------------------------

Item 5. ----------------------------

A. poor communicator

B. unpunctual

C. untidy

D. unfriendly

E. lazy

F. disorganized

G. unreliable

H. bossy

II. Listen to the five recordings again and choose the best answers to the questions you hear.

1. A. He is not fond of paperwork.　　　　B. He is careful about his appearance.

C. He is untidy in his work space.　　　　D. He is not serious about his work.

2. A. Jerome is his superior.　　　　B. Jerome is his inferior.

C. Jerome is his peer.　　　　D. Jerome is his client.

3. A. Joking and chatting in the office.　　　　B. Painting her nails in the office.

C. Interfering with her colleagues' work.　　　　D. Delaying her work until deadlines fall.

4. A. He is rather reserved and doesn't communicate well with the staff.

B. He has no idea what problems the company is having at the moment.

C. He is so lenient with the staff that few people pay attention to his words.

D. He only criticizes but fails to explain how the staff can help to improve.

5. A. George's colleagues are accustomed to his being unpunctual.

B. George's PA never reminds him to get to the meeting on time.

C. George's PA always gets the time for meeting confused.

D. George is late as he has to drive his family to the airport.

Home Listening

Business News

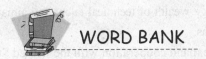

WORD BANK

nanotechnology	/ˌnænəʊtekˈnɒlədʒɪ/	*n.*	纳米技术
hub	/hʌb/	*n.*	中心
hamper	/ˈhæmpə/	*v.*	妨碍，阻碍
impediment	/ɪmˈpedɪmənt/	*n.*	妨碍，阻碍
subsidy	/ˈsʌbsɪdɪ/	*n.*	补助金，津贴
outsource	/ˈaʊtsɔːs/	*v.*	把（如工作等）包给外面的供应者或生产者
come of age			成熟，发达
phase out			逐步淘汰
New Delhi	/njuːˈdeli/		新德里（印度首都）

Listen to the business news report and choose the best answers to the questions you hear.

1. A. Before India conducted nuclear weapons tests.

   B. After India conducted nuclear weapons tests.

   C. Before India refused to give American agricultural goods freer access to its markets.

   D. After India refused to give American agricultural goods freer access to its markets.

2. A. In the field of life sciences.

   B. In the field of nanotechnology.

   C. In the field of civilian space development.

   D. In the field of military space development.

3. A. India set up trade barriers against US exports on dual-technology.

   B. In spite of US opposition, India conducted nuclear weapons tests in 1998.

   C. Indians working in the United States are taking away job opportunities from Americans.

   D. India is reluctant to break down trade barriers and give American agricultural goods freer access to its markets.

4. A. The IT sector is still an infant industry in India and will take off with more government regulation and support.

B. India boasts of a huge wealth of technical talent and aims at becoming a major research center in various areas.

C. India is seeking to expand cooperation with the United States in high-technology trade by removing some trade barriers.

D. India holds that developing countries can increase developed countries' access to their markets if developed countries agree to cancel farm subsidies.

5. A. Dual-use technology refers to knowledge-based technologies that are intended for military applications.

B. Dual-technology products were barred to India because they could be applied to both civilian and military industries.

C. Indian exports to the States grew by 25 percent this year as a result of recent tariff reductions by the Indian government.

D. Farmers in poor regions are receiving government subsidies in order to increase the competitiveness of their produce in the global market.

Unit 9

Company

Dictation

Listen to the following short paragraph and fill in the blanks with what you hear.

A multinational corporation is a business enterprise with (1) _____ _____ in one or more foreign countries. Typically, a multinational corporation develops new products (2) _____ and manufactures them abroad, thus gaining trade advantages and (3) _____ and materials. Almost all the largest multinational firms are (4) _____ _____. Such corporations have had worldwide influence — (5) _____ _____ and even over governments, many of which have imposed controls on them. Proponents of such enterprises maintain that they (6) _____ _____, and improve technology in countries that are in need of such development. Critics, however, point to their political influence, their (7) _____ _____, and (8) _____ which results in the corporations' home countries.

Listening & Speaking

SECTION A **Multinational Corporations**

Pre-listening ▶▶▶

Discussion

Discuss the following questions with your partner and take notes when necessary.

1. Can you mention some of the multinational corporations that have business operations in your area?

   ----

2. How do you like the prospect of working in a multinational corporation?

Listening ▶▶▶

Conversation

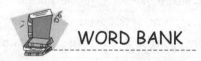

WORD BANK

| expertise | /ˌekspɜːˈtiːz/ | *n.* | 专业知识 |
| incorporate | /ɪnˈkɔːpəreɪt/ | *v.* | 组成公司，注册成立 |

Liberia	/laɪˈbɪərɪə/	*n.*	利比亚
multinational	/ˌmʌltɪˈnæʃən(ə)l/	*a.*	跨国的，多国的
convinced	/kənˈvɪnst/	*a.*	信服的，确信的
be subject to			遵守

I. Listen to the conversation and answer the following questions in your own words.

1. What is the relationship between the two speakers?

   _____

2. What are they mainly talking about?

   _____

3. What is Mrs. Watt's reaction to the big news?

   _____

4. Why are they going to make the business trip?

   _____

5. How does Mr. Thompson define his company?

   _____

6. Why do industries such as shipbuilding, aircraft, and automobiles have to explore overseas markets?

   _____

7. How does Mrs. Watt think of internationalism?

   _____

8. How are nations tied to each other according to Mr. Thompson?

   _____

II. Listen to the conversation again and complete the notes with what you hear.

Company Profile

Place of birth: _____

Company Scale:

Our company boasts of:
✓ 126 _____
✓ 13 _____
✓ 8 _____
✓ 125,000 _____
✓ over 30 _____
✓ 30 _____
✓ half of the net income coming from _____

Passage

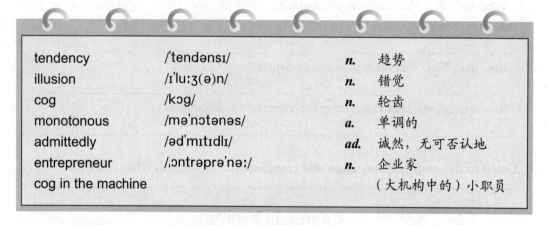

WORD BANK

tendency	/ˈtendənsɪ/	*n.*	趋势
illusion	/ɪˈluːʒ(ə)n/	*n.*	错觉
cog	/kɒg/	*n.*	轮齿
monotonous	/məˈnɒtənəs/	*a.*	单调的
admittedly	/ədˈmɪtɪdlɪ/	*ad.*	诚然，无可否认地
entrepreneur	/ˌɒntrəprəˈnəː/	*n.*	企业家
cog in the machine			（大机构中的）小职员

I. Listen to the passage and answer the following questions in your own words.

1. What does the passage mainly talk about?

_____

2. How does the speaker feel about the college graduates' preference for big companies?

_____

3. In terms of company size, what type of companies does the speaker prefer to work for?

_____

4. What may arouse your sense of responsibility when you are working?

_____

5. What is crucial to the development of your ability to work?

_____

6. How does the speaker feel about working in big companies?

_____

II. Listen to the passage again and complete the notes with what you hear.

	Big Companies	Small Companies
Fame	provided with (1) _____ _____; enjoying (2)_____ _____ of the company	
Working Role	working as (3) _____ _____	having more decisions to make; being able to see (4) _____ _____ right away
Career Advancement	having little chances to (5) _____ _____	exposed to (6) _____ _____; expected to do more things than in a large company
Welfare	enjoying (7) _____ _____	earning a bit lower salary
Job Satisfaction	doing (8) _____ job; doing demanding and competitive work; suffering (9) _____ to outperform fellow-competitors	feeling more (10) _____ _____; working comfortably and feeling at ease

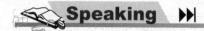
Speaking ▶▶

Discussion & Debate

• •

Nowadays it is not uncommon for college graduates to give up well-paid jobs in big companies in exchange for less-paid, but less-demanding ones in order to "enjoy life more". How do you think about this phenomenon? Let's have a debate.

☎ **Work as a class. Divide the class into two sides. Side A holds that those people have good reasons to justify their choice and Side B argues that those people are mere failures and they are just using it as an excuse to escape from the pressure in the job field.**

☎ **Work in groups. Make groups of four to six. Half of the groups will take the side of A and the other half will side with B. Have a pre-debate discussion. Each group prepares its arguments and supporting facts by brainstorming together.**

☎ **Work as a class. Start the debate. It is arranged in such a way that a debate takes place between the two groups holding opposite views and goes on until one side fails to retort.**

 **Start-up Companies**

Pre-listening ▶▶

Discussion

• •

Discuss the following questions with your partner and take notes when necessary.

1. How do you like the idea of starting a business of your own?

----

2. What do you know about the procedure for registration of a company in China?

Listening ▶▶

Conversation

● ●

WORD BANK

solicitor	/səˈlɪsɪtə(r)/	*n.*	律师
registrar	/ˌredʒɪsˈtrɑː/	*n.*	注册登记员
objection	/əbˈdʒekʃən/	*n.*	反对
liability	/ˌlaɪəˈbɪlɪtɪ/	*n.*	责任
straightforward	/streɪtˈfɔːwəd/	*a.*	简明的，易懂的
provision	/prəˈvɪʒ(ə)n/	*n.*	规定，条款
deal in			经营，交易
memorandum of association			公司章程
articles of association			公司管理规则
the Companies Act			公司法
managing director			常务董事，总经理

I. Listen to the conversation and decide whether the following statements are true or false. Write T for true and F for false in the brackets.

1. (   ) The speakers are talking on the phone about the registration of their company.

2. (   ) The name of the company was proposed by the solicitor.

3. (   ) It is not allowable to pick a company name which is like that of any other company on the Register.

4. (   ) All the business of the company will be restricted to Hong Kong.

5. (   ) The type of the company is demonstrated in the articles of association.

6. (   ) The company will be guided by the regulations of the Companies Act.

7. (   ) The requirements for the management of the company are covered in the articles of association.

8. (   ) Mr. Taylor will have to be a shareholder of the company.

9. (   ) A private limited company refers to one whose members hold limited liability.

10. (   ) Mr. Taylor will have to appoint a managing director of the company before registration.

II. Listen to the conversation again and complete the answers to the questions below.

1. What does the memorandum of association contain?

The memorandum of association contains the following items.

❑ (1) _____.

❑ The location of the registered office: (2) _____.

❑ The objectives of the company: "(3) _____"
and "(4) _____".

❑ The type of the company: (5) _____.

❑ (6) _____.

❑ The number of the shares it is divided into.

2. How is the issue of directors stipulated in the articles of association?

❑ A private company only needs to have (7) _____ and he
doesn't have to be (8) _____.

❑ A director may also be the secretary, but not if (9) _____.

❑ Mr. Taylor can act as (10) _____.

Passage

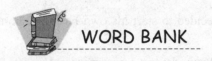

WORD BANK

dropout	/'drɒpaʊt/	*n.*	退学学生
brainstorm	/'breɪnstɔːm/	*v.*	集体讨论
hobbyist	/'hɒbɪɪst/	*n.*	沉溺于某种癖好者
prototype	/'prəʊtəʊtaɪp/	*n.*	原型，样机（品）
trio	/'triːəʊ/	*n.*	三人一组
undertaking	/ˌʌndə'teɪkɪŋ/	*n.*	事业
drum up			招徕，唤起
circuit board			电路板
Hewlett Packard			惠普公司

I. Listen to the passage and choose the best answers to the questions you hear.

1. A. To repair electronic boards.

   B. To design electronic games.

   C. To produce circuit boards and sell them.

   D. To make electronic game players and sell them.

2. A. He acted as the accountant.   B. He acted as the shareholder.

   C. He acted as the fund collector.   D. He acted as the benefactor.

3. A. An electronic hobbyist.   B. The owner of a hobby shop.

   C. A personal computer owner.   D. One of their friends.

4. A. In 1975.   B. In 1976.   C. In 1977.   D. In 1978.

5. A. He hoped that it would be as much favored as apples.

   B. He acknowledged that it was the fruit of their collective wisdom.

   C. He intended to express the spiritual nature of their business.

D. He believed that it would bring them more good luck.

II. Listen to the passage again and decide whether the following statements are true or false. Write T for true and F for false in the brackets.

1. (   ) Steve Jobs decided to start his own business shortly after he graduated from the college.

2. (   ) It was when he worked as a repairman at Hewlett Packard that Steve Wozniak had the idea of making and selling circuit boards.

3. (   ) In the 1970s, the computer game was beginning to become popular among Americans.

4. (   ) It only took Apple's founders quite a short time to bring out their first prototype.

5. (   ) Apple Computer was founded by Steve Jobs, Steve Wozniak, and Ron Wayne in April 1, 1976.

6. (   ) Steve and his trio earned $500 for each of the circuit board they sold in their first deal.

7. (   ) Bill Gates started his "very own" software company in the same year when Apple was established.

8. (   ) Steve Jobs and Steve Wozniak decided to name their business Apple after some heated discussions.

9. (   ) Bill Gates accepted Apple's job offer and worked as a computer programmer there in 1977 as he was in bad need of money then.

10. (   ) At the start very few people envisioned the success of Apple.

 **Speaking** ▶▶

Story-telling

☎ **Work in groups. Discuss the picture with the help of the questions provided below.**

■ Who are these people?

■ Where are they?

■ What are they doing?

■ What will they do next?

■ What does the caption under the picture mean?

■ What does the caption under the picture suggest?

☎ Work in groups. Make up a story according to what you read from the picture. Try to make your story as dramatic as possible.

☎ Work as a class. Share your story with the rest of the class. Then pick up your favorite story and tell why you love it most.

"Get ready, guys! Another 10 minutes
and we no longer can be considered a
'start-up.'"

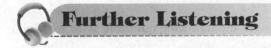 **Further Listening**

Short Recordings

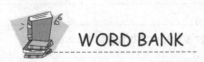 WORD BANK

| delegate | /ˈdelɪɡət/ | *n.* | 代表 |
| due | /djuː/ | *a.* | 应到的，预期的 |

catering	/ˈkeɪtərɪŋ/	*n.*	（会议或社交活动的）饮食服务
technophobe	/ˌteknəʊˈfəʊb/	*n.*	对新技术有恐惧的人
book	/bʊk/	*n.*	（常用复数）账簿
overdraw	/ˌəʊvəˈdrɔː/	*v.*	透支
sort out			解决

I. In this section, you will hear five short recordings. For each piece, decide what the speaker's job is.

Item 1.   ----------------------
Item 2.   ----------------------
Item 3.   ----------------------
Item 4.   ----------------------
Item 5.   ----------------------

A. Conference organizer
B. Personal assistant
C. Chief executive
D. Warehouse manager
E. Personnel officer
F. Accounts clerk
G. Software technician
H. Hotel receptionist

II. Listen to the five recordings again and answer the following questions with what you hear.

1. What does the first speaker enjoy about her work?

_____

2. How did the second speaker deal with the disappearing of the catering staff?

_____

_____

3. What is the third speaker's responsibility at the company?

_____

_____

4. For what problems did many people use to call the fourth speaker for help?

_____

_____

_____

5. What does the fifth speaker's job involve?

_____

_____

Home Listening

Business News

WORD BANK

attribute	/əˈtrɪbju(ː)t/	*v.*	归结于
staffer	/ˈstɑːfə(r)/	*n.*	职员
Merrill Lynch			美林公司（国际著名金融投资管理公司，现已经被美国银行收购）
Japan Franchise Association			日本特许经营权协会
Starbucks			星巴克（全球最大的咖啡零售经销商）

Listen to the business news report and decide whether the following statements are true or false. Write T for true and F for false in the brackets.

1. (   ) Foreign direct investment in Japan is booming while Japan's overseas investment is going down.

2. (   ) Summer is a slack business season for products such as cold beverages and ice cream because it is typical of Japan to have cool weather in summer.

3. (   ) More Japanese companies are setting up factories in China to take advantage of

cheaper labor there.

4. (   ) The difficult conditions in Japan's home market are holding back foreign enthusiasm for investment in Japan.

5. (   ) With foreign direct investment heating up in Japan, sales in Japanese convenience stores were also on the increase.

6. (   ) Owing to tense competition, the number of Starbucks outlets in Japan would be reduced.

7. (   ) Starbucks Coffee Japan reported a decline of $380,000 in its net profit the first quarter of the fiscal year.

8. (   ) Toyota, Japan's largest automaker, is offering its employees free family cars to reduce traffic jams.

Unit **10**

• **Payment**

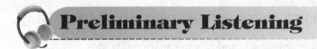
Dictation

Listen to the following short paragraph and fill in the blanks with what you hear.

A payment is the (1) _____ from one party (such as a person or company) to another. A payment is usually made in exchange for (2) _____ _____, services, or both, or to (3) _____.
The simplest and oldest form of payment is barter, the exchange of one good or service for another. In the modern world, common means of payment by an individual include (4) _____, and in trade such payments are frequently (5) _____ or result in a receipt. However, there are no (6) _____ on the form a payment can take and thus in (7) _____ between businesses, payments may take the form of stock or other more (8) _____.

Listening & Speaking

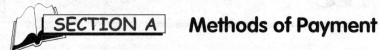

SECTION A   **Methods of Payment**

Pre-listening ▶▶

Discussion

Discuss the following questions with your partner and take notes when necessary.

1. What methods of payment are usually employed in today's international trade?

....

....

2. If you are the seller, what concerns you most in terms of international payment? How could you best protect your interests in the transaction? And what if you are the buyer?

....

....

Listening ▶▶

Conversation

WORD BANK

expire	/ɪkˈspaɪə(r)/	*v.*	到期

validity	/vəˈlɪdɪtɪ/	*n.*	有效期
irrevocable	/ɪˈrevəkəbl/	*a.*	不可撤销的
transshipment	/trænsˈʃɪpmənt/	*n.*	转船
amend	/əˈmend/	*v.*	改正，修改
conformity	/kənˈfɔːmɪtɪ/	*n.*	一致，符合
amendment	/əˈmendmənt/	*n.*	改正，修改
run counter to			与……相反，不一致
CIF			（Cost, Insurance and Freight）到岸价格（成本、保险费加运费）
Freight to Collect			运费到付

I. Listen to the conversation and choose the best answers to the questions you hear.

1. A. Shipment should be effected in September or October.

   B. Shipment should be effected no later than the 20th of October.

   C. Shipment should be effected before the 31st of October.

   D. Shipment should be effected on the 5th of November.

2. A. Commercial invoice.   B. Ocean Bill of Lading.

   C. Insurance policy.   D. Packing list.

3. A. The expiry date of the amended L/C should be on the 5th of November.

   B. The latest shipment date should be extended to the 31st of October.

   C. The amended L/C should be revocable and transferable.

   D. The amended L/C should bear the mark of "Freight to Collect".

4. A. It allows both partial shipment and transshipment.

   B. It only allows transshipment.

   C. It only allows partial shipment.

   D. It allows neither partial shipment nor transshipment.

5. A. Mr. Martin's company may suffer losses caused by the delay.

   B. Mr. Martin's company will be held responsible for the delay.

   C. Mr. Martin's company will be advised to extend the validity.

   D. Mr. Martin's company will claim on the insurer for the losses.

II. Listen to the conversation again and complete the following amended Letter of Credit according to the advice given by Mr. Martin.

JC Logistics Corporation

OUR ADVICE NUMBER: EA 00000091   -------- AMMOUNT-------

ADVICE DATE: 08OCT2004

ISSUING BANK REF: 3312/HBI/22341   USD25,000,000

EXPIRY DATE: (1) _____

BENEFICIARY: APPLICANT:

THE WALTON SUPPLY CO.   JC LOGISTICS CORPORATION

2356 SOUTH N.W. STREET   34 INDUSTRIAL DRIVE

ATLANTA, GEORGIA, 30345   CENTRAL, HONGKONG

WE HAVE BEEN REQUESTED TO ADVISE TO YOU THE FOLLOWING LETTER OF CREDIT AS ISSUED BY THIRD HONGKONG BANK

PLEASE BE GUIDED BY ITS TERMS AND CONDITIONS AND BY THE FOLLOWING:

CREDIT IS AVAILABLE UNDER THE CONTRACT (2) _____

SIGHT FOR 100 PERCENT OF INVOICE VALUE DRAWN ON US ACCOMPANIED BY THE FOLLOWING DOCUMENTS:

1. (3) _____ IN 1 ORIGINAL AND 3 COPIES

2. (4) _____ CONSIGNED TO THE ORDER OF THIRD HONGKONG BANK

3. (5) PACKING LIST IN _____

EVIDENCING SHIPMENT OF 5000 PINE LOGS—WHOLE—12/8 FEET

PRICE TERMS: (6) _____ (CIF/CFR/FOB) GEORGIA

SHIPMENT FROM: SAVANNAH, GEORGIA   TO: HONGKONG

LATEST SHIPPING DATE: (7) _____

(8) _____ ALLOWED

AT THE REQUEST OF OUR CORRESPONDENT, WE CONFIRM THIS CREDIT.

THIS LETTER OF CREDIT IS (9) _____.

PLEASE EXAMINE THIS ISTRUMENT CAREFULLY. IF YOU ARE UNABLE TO COMPLY WITH THE TERMS OR CONDITIONS, PLEASE COMMUNICATE YOUR BUYER TO ARRANGE FOR AN AMMENDMENT.

Passage

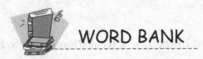

WORD BANK

minimize	/ˈmɪnɪmaɪz/	*v.*	将……减到最少，最小化
undertaking	/ˌʌndəˈteɪkɪŋ/	*n.*	承诺，保证
beneficiary	/ˌbenɪˈfɪʃ ərɪ/	*n.*	受益人
presentation	/ˌprezənˈteɪʃ(ə)n/	*n.*	（支票的）提出，交兑
underlying	/ˌʌndəˈlaɪɪŋ/	*a.*	潜在的
regulation	/ˌregjʊˈleɪʃ ən/	*n.*	规定
rejection	/rɪˈdʒekʃ ən/	*n.*	拒付
comply with			遵守

I. Listen to the passage and decide whether the following statements are true or false. Write T for true and F for false in the brackets.

1. (   ) The methods of payment used are mainly decided by economic conditions, commercial risk and political risk of the exporting country.

2. (   ) The risks involved in exporting can be reduced depending on the method of payment arranged with the exporter, the importer and the bank.

3. (   ) Letter of Credit is a safe method of payment to both the importer and the exporter.

4. (   ) The exporter will effect the payment only if the terms of the credit are met precisely.

5. (   ) It is the exporter's obligation to apply for a Letter of Credit to be issued.

6. (   ) In order to avoid rejections, the exporter must ensure the credit properly represents the sales contract.

7. (   ) Letter of Credit is much safer than the cash payment in international trade as long as the terms of the credit are met.

8. (   ) What all parties in the letter of credit transaction deal with are physical goods instead of documents.

II. **Listen to the passage again and complete the following L/C circulation chart with what you hear.**

Parties Involved in the L/C Circulation & Their Responsibilities

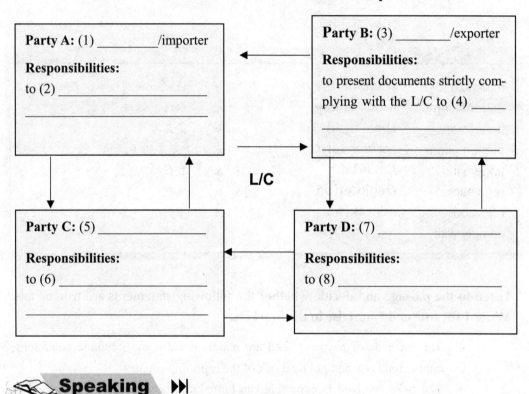

Party A: (1) _____/importer

Responsibilities:

to (2) _____

_____

Party B: (3) _____/exporter

Responsibilities:

to present documents strictly complying with the L/C to (4) _____

_____

_____

L/C

Party C: (5) _____

Responsibilities:

to (6) _____

_____

Party D: (7) _____

Responsibilities:

to (8) _____

_____

Speaking ▶▶

Discussion

☎ **Work in groups. Read the advertisement here below for a business book club. Discuss with your group over the plus and minus of payment alternatives suggested in the advertisement and decide which mode of daily payment you would prefer.**

☎ **Work as a class. Compare and share your insights with the rest of the class.**

Join the Business Book Club!

We will send you a new book, monthly, from our fantastic range of business books. Managers all over the world read these books and their business gets better and better.

There is no need to pay immediately. Look at the books and if you like them, we will send you a bill. If you do not want the book, send it back in the box provided.

Join the business book club is simple.

We will need details of your bank account and you can pay by automatic bank transfer, by check, by credit card or with cash. It's really simple. If you want to discuss payment terms, call us now on:

01713894562

Books written by managers for managers! Don't delay, join TODAY!

Daily Payment	Plus	Minus
By bank transfer		
By check		
By credit card		
By cash		

Your payment preference (State your reasons briefly):

SECTION B E-payment

Pre-listening ▶▶

Discussion

•••

Discuss the following questions with your partner and take notes when necessary.

1. How has money evolved in its form? And what form do you think money of the future will take?

----

2. Do you like to make your payments with credit cards? Why or why not?

Listening ▶▶

Conversation

•••

WORD BANK

| transaction | /trænˈzækʃ(ə)n/ | n. | 交易 |
| encrypt | /ɪnˈkrɪpt/ | v. | 设置密码 |

pal	/pæl/	*n.*	<口> 好朋友，伙伴
buck	/bʌk/		<口> 美元
elaborate on			详细解释

I. Listen to the conversation and choose the best answers to the questions you hear.

1. A. It refers to payment via the telephone. B. It refers to payment by bank notes.
   C. It refers to payment in an easy manner. D. It refers to payment in the electronic way.

2. A. They are still not very reliable. B. They are already in operation.
   C. They are used only on trial. D. They are used on a small scale.

3. A. The time of transaction. B. The total value of transaction.
   C. The buyer's credit rating. D. The buyer's credit card number.

4. A. By e-payment, transaction information is transmitted through the Internet.
   B. By e-payment, transaction information is exchanged via the telephone.
   C. By e-payment, transaction information should be confirmed by the bank.
   D. By e-payment, transaction information is encrypted for the sake of security.

5. A. E-payment will lead to the phase-out of cash and bank notes.
   B. E-payment will improve the cash flow of the merchant.
   C. E-payment may arouse people's concern over payment security.
   D. E-payment will save transaction expenses for all the parties involved.

II. Listen to the conversation again and complete the chart with what you hear.

E-PAYMENT KNOW-HOW		
Parties Involved	A: Customer	➤ give (1) _____ to Party B
	B: (2) _____	➤ send (3) _____ to Party C ➤ receive (4) _____ from Party C
	C: (5) _____	➤ receive the related information ➤ adjust (6) _____
Advantage(s)	Compared with traditional payment, E-payment is ➤ (7) _____. ➤ (8) _____.	

continued

E-PAYMENT KNOW-HOW	
Advantage(s)	For example: ➤ E-payment can be used by (9) _____. ➤ E-payment can be used for (10) _____ _____.
Disadvantage(s)	Major security concerns: ➤ clients' money may (11) _____ _____. ➤ computer system may (12) _____.

Passage

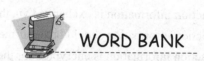

WORD BANK

denominator	/dɪˈnɔmɪneɪtə(r)/	*n.*	标准，衡量的尺度
deferred	/dɪˈfəːd/	*a.*	推迟的，延期的
entity	/ˈentɪtɪ/	*n.*	实体，独立存在体
infrastructure	/ˌɪnfrəˈstrʌktʃə(r)/	*n.*	基础设施
monopoly	/məˈnɔpəlɪ/	*v.*	垄断
charter	/ˈtʃɑːtə(r)/	*v.*	租用，包租
multiplicity	/ˌmʌltɪˈplɪsɪtɪ/	*n.*	多样性
guise	/gaɪz/	*n.*	外表，伪装
zap	/zæp/	*v.*	快速移动；快速转账
greenback	/ˈgriːnbæk/	*n.*	美钞
Federal Reserve Bank			联邦储备银行

I. Listen to the passage and choose the best answers to the questions you hear.

1. A. Stone.   B. Shell.   C. Sugar.   D. Slave.

2. A. Money can be used to store the current value of different commodities.

   B. Money can be used to measure the values of goods and delay the payment.

   C. Money can be used to expedite the conclusion of a business transaction.

   D. Money can be used as a standard that enables trade to take place in the future.

3. A. Only local governments.

   B. Only central governments.

   C. Both central banks and the private banks.

   D. Local governments, private banks as well as other institutions.

4. A. Digital money takes various forms.

   B. Digital money is issued by central banks.

   C. Digital money is quite complex for daily use.

   D. Digital money must be backed by gold or silver.

5. A. The major functions of money.

   B. The various forms of money.

   C. The advantages of e-cash over paper money.

   D. The development of money through history.

II. Listen to the passage again and complete the notes with what you hear.

About Money

Throughout history, money took forms of both metals and other objects such as (1) _____ _____ . In the modern world money consists of (2) _____ . In the early stage, money was flexible and exchanged in many ways. But objects such as seashells, stones were gradually replaced by (3) _____ and these in turn replaced by paper money. Later, many countries issued their national currencies and monopolized the money system so that money systems tend to (4) _____ . As a result the transaction of money will take a lot of time and expenses. Developing with the technology, money takes the new form of (5) _____

_____ that moves through many forms of networks. It is the ultimate and inevitable currency for the wired world with the advantages of (6) _____. However, no matter the changes in its form, money's functions remain the same: a (7) _____ and a (8) _____.

Speaking ▶▶

Debate

☎ Work alone. As e-money gains in popularity, some people forecast hopefully that in the quite near future digital money will wipe out the conventional money we are using today and our society will go cashless one day. Think and decide whether you agree with this view or not.

☎ Work as a class. Divide the class into two sides (the pros and the cons) and debate over the possibility of a cashless society in the future. Work out as many arguments as possible with your fellow students to defend your side.

Will our society go cashless one day?	
The Pros	The Cons
☐ Cash is inconvenient to carry about;	☐ E-money is not secure;
☐	☐
☐	☐
☐	☐

Further Listening

Short Recordings

WORD BANK

sophisticated	/səˈfɪstɪkeɪtɪd/	*a.*	高度发展的；精密复杂的
visually	/ˈvɪʒuəlɪ/	*ad.*	视觉上地，直观地
incredibly	/ɪnˈkredəblɪ/	*ad.*	难以置信地，不可思议地
premium	/ˈpriːmɪəm/	*n.*	保险费
dire	/ˈdaɪə(r)/	*a.*	可怕的
reputation	/ˌrepjuˈteɪʃ(ə)n/	*n.*	名誉，声望
assessment	/əˈsesmənt/	*n.*	评估，估算
tailor-made	/ˈteɪləˈmeɪd/	*a.*	特制的，定做的
balance sheet			资产负债表

I. **In this section, you will hear five short recordings. For each piece, decide what sort of service the company offers.**

Item 1. ....

Item 2. ....

Item 3. ....

Item 4. ....

Item 5. ....

A. management consultancy

B. website design

C. insurance

D. banking

E. catering

F. advertising

G. travel

H. telecommunications

II. Listen to the five recordings again and choose the best answers to the questions you hear.

1. A. Seniority and communication skills are much valued in his line.

   B. His line of work requires creativity and refined technical skills.

   C. Companies are reluctant to recognize the effectiveness of their work.

   D. People in his line usually work with the marketing staff of a company.

2. A. Soaring fuel price.   B. Rising insurance cost.

   C. Fierce market competition.   D. Uncertain financial markets.

3. A. Because people need his service only when they have to pay out the premiums.

   B. Because people need his service only when they want to buy daily necessities.

   C. Because people need his service only when something unfortunate happens to them.

   D. Because people need his service only when they lose their valuables on holiday.

4. A. Building corporate reputation.   B. Providing practical solutions.

   C. Evaluating risk factors.   D. Facilitating risk management.

5. A. Proper system maintenance.   B. High system security.

   C. Worldwide coverage.   D. All of the above.

Home Listening

Business News

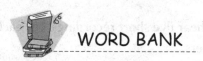

WORD BANK

tumble	/ˈtʌmbl/	*v.*	（证券价格等）下跌
session	/ˈseʃən/	*n.*	（证券等的）一次交易
paralysis	/pəˈrælɪsɪs/	*n.*	瘫痪，麻痹
unload	/ʌnˈləud/	*v.*	抛售（证券）
recall	/rɪˈkɔːl/	*v.*	召回

macro	/ˈmækrəu/	**a.**	巨大的，特别突出的
take its toll			造成损失
mad cow disease			疯牛病（医学上称为牛脑海绵状病）
Goldman Sachs			高盛公司（美国一家著名的市场投资及预测公司）

Listen to the news report and decide whether the following statements are true or false. Write T for true and F for false in the brackets.

1. (   ) As a rule, the US stock market fluctuates considerably during the session on the day before the Christmas holiday.

2. (   ) US stocks slumped on Wednesday after the first US case of mad cow disease was convinced by the US Department of Agriculture.

3. (   ) Americans feel disturbed by the discovery of the mad cow case because the diseased beef is dangerous for human consumption.

4. (   ) McDonalds, Wendy's, Outback Steakhouse, and Tyson are all US restaurant giants specializing in hamburgers and steak.

5. (   ) Officials in Washington, D.C. have already called back approximately 7,000 kilograms of beef.

6. (   ) According to recent reports, the US economy as a whole has been affected by the mad cow crisis, which is rocking its beef industry.

7. (   ) Japan, Mexico, Russia and South Korea, along with Britain, have stopped importing US beef when the mad cow disease was diagnosed.

8. (   ) Chicken, pork and beef fall into the category of white meat, while seafood is not under the same umbrella.

 **Unit 11**

Competition

Dictation

Listen to the following short paragraph and fill in the blanks with what you hear.

Competition is the battle between businesses to win (1) _____
_____. The free-enterprise system ensures businesses make decisions
about what to produce, how to produce it, and (2) _____
_____. Competition is a (3) _____
_____ because it is believed that having more than one
business competing for the same consumers will cause the products or services to be
provided at (4) _____ than if there were no
competitors. To be successful in today's competitive business world, it is important for
businesses to be aware of (5) _____ and to find
a way to (6) _____ on the competitors' product or
service. It is also important to pay attention to (7) _____
_____ and to (8) _____ before the competition does.

Listening & Speaking

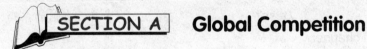

SECTION A   **Global Competition**

Pre-listening ▶▶

Discussion

••

Discuss the following questions with your partner and take notes when necessary.

1. What industries are undergoing the fiercest competition in today's global market?

----

2. How can Chinese enterprises manage to win out in the global competition?

Listening ▶▶

Conversation

••

WORD BANK

| fold | /fəʊld/ | *v.* | 失败；关停 |
| hinder | /ˈhɪndə(r)/ | *v.* | 阻碍，打扰 |

cultivate	/ˈkʌltɪveɪt/	*v.*	培养
reallocate	/riːˈæləkeɪt/	*v.*	再分配，再指派
asset	/ˈæset/	*n.*	资产；有用的东西
distribution channel			销售渠道

I. Listen to the conversation and decide whether the following statements are true or false. Write T for true and F for false in the brackets.

1. (   ) After China's entry into the WTO, the whole China market will be open to global competition to an even greater extent.

2. (   ) After China's entry into the WTO, all the Chinese companies will face the challenge of being folded out from the heated competition market.

3. (   ) Low price policy is a two-edged competition as it is a way to seize customers at the sacrifice of the development of the whole industry.

4. (   ) It is suggested that Chinese companies should put more efforts on promoting their brand image.

5. (   ) Brand competition is a new challenge to most Chinese companies and if they fail to handle it properly, they are likely to lose their leading position to foreigner competitors.

6. (   ) In current China market, the competition between foreign brands and local brands has replaced that among local brands.

7. (   ) Many Chinese customers are likely to accept foreign brands for their good brand images.

8. (   ) On the whole, the interviewee is quite pessimistic about the Chinese industry and its future development after China's WTO entry.

II. Listen to the conversation again and complete the notes with what you hear.

Opportunities along with Challenges

The Whole Picture

After entry into the WTO:

❑ businesses of (1) _____ will be out of the market.

❑ companies with (2) _____ ,
(3) _____ and (4) _____ will
win more market share.

Challenges

❑ (5) _____ .
❑ (6) _____ .
❑ (7) _____ .
❑ (8) _____ .

Ways to Strengthen the Competitive Advantages

❑ Further improve (9) _____ , (10) _____ ,
and be creative in (11) _____ , and (12) _____
_____ .
❑ Actively introduce and learn (13) _____ ,
and cultivate (14) _____ .
❑ Reallocate (15) _____ .

Passage

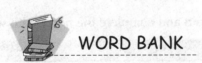

WORD BANK

overlook	/ˌəʊvəˈlʊk/	*v.*	没注意到
prospect	/ˈprɒspekt/	*n.*	<美> 可能成为主顾的人
niche	/nɪtʃ/	*n.*	商机；市场定位
insight	/ˈɪnsaɪt/	*n.*	洞察力，见识

testimonial	/ˌtestɪˈməʊnɪəl/	n.	推荐
endorsement	/ɪnˈdɔːsmənt/	n.	认可；背书
niche market			缝隙市场

I. Listen to the passage and decide whether the following statements are mentioned or not. Put a tick before those that are mentioned.

1. (   ) Competition can be found everywhere in the world.

2. (   ) Unconventional marketing methods refers to methods which are different from those used by other businessmen.

3. (   ) When it comes to marketing, it is important to identify a target audience and cater to their needs.

4. (   ) The larger audience you target at, the more likely you will profit.

5. (   ) Customers tend to be incredulous about specialists and their recommendations.

6. (   ) According to the passage, if you target at the right customers with the right marketing methods, you are likely to avoid competition.

7. (   ) Comments made by customers are more reliable than specialist recommendations.

8. (   ) Specialist marketing can be applied to the products where a business's special strength lies.

9. (   ) Uniqueness is most essential when marketing a product.

10. (   ) To establish yourself as a specialist in your business area, you should replace your current marketing with unconventional marketing.

II. Listen to the passage again and complete the notes with what you hear.

Competition Is Everywhere

Ways to minimize the impact of competition:
✎ (1) _____.
✎ (2) _____.

✏ (3) _____ .

How to appeal to the niche market

✏ for stay-at-home moms: (4) _____

✏ for corporate employees: (5) _____

_____ .

✏ for retirees: (6) _____

_____ .

Speaking ▶▶|

Discussion

● ●

☎ **Work in groups. Name a leading domestic brand in each of the following industries, and then list its major competitors in the market, both domestic and foreign.**

Industry	Leading Domestic Brand	Major Domestic Competitors	Major Foreign Competitors
Household appliances			
Retailing			
Computer			
Dairy			
Leisure/Sports Wear			
Automobile			
Banking			
Mobile phone			
Cosmetics			
Drinks & beverage			

☎ **Work in groups. Pick one brand you are most familiar with and discuss:**

1. How competitive the brand is in the local and global market?
2. What can be done to enhance the competition ability of the brand in the local and global market?

☎ **Work as a class. Each group presents its findings to the rest of the class.**

SECTION B **Fair Competition**

Pre-listening ▶▶

Discussion

Discuss the following questions with your partner and take notes when necessary.

1. How does market competition impact the growth of a business?

----

2. Can fair play go along with business competition? Why or why not?

Listening ▶▶

Conversation

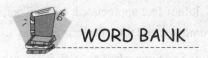

WORD BANK

retain	/rɪˈteɪn/	*v.*	保持，保留
forge	/fɔːdʒ/	*v.*	铸造
facilitate	/fəˈsɪlɪteɪt/	*v.*	推动，促进
segment	/ˈsegmənt/	*v.*	分割，区分
compassionate	/kəmˈpæʃənɪt/	*a.*	富于同情心的
affirm	/əˈfɜːm/	*v.*	肯定
retention	/rɪˈtenʃən/	*n.*	保持力；存留
demoralize	/dɪˈmɔrəlaɪz/	*v.*	士气受挫
talent pool			人才库

I. Listen to the conversation and decide whether the following statements are true or false. Write T for true and F for false in the brackets.

1. (   ) The interviewee elaborated on the effect of "war for talent" on the global economy.

2. (   ) It is predicted that the shortage of managerial talent will last over the next twenty years at least.

3. (   ) General Electric has long been admired for the strength and depth of its technical talent.

4. (   ) Most companies give talent building priority as they have come to realize the linkage between talent management and business performance.

5. (   ) Talent is considered a critical driver of corporate performance and a prerequisite to the implementation of other performance drives.

6. (   ) Based on their performance, employees should be treated differently in respect of the pay, opportunities, and other investments made in them.

7. (   ) Fair and compassionate corporate leaders tend to consider every employee equally talented and treat them in the same way.

8. (   ) If employees do not feel appreciated, recognized, and valued, they are likely to leave the company, and their performance invariably suffers.

9. (   ) Staff affirmation is as important as staff differentiation in managing corporate talent more effectively.

10. (   ) The first step for companies to better talent management is to think of talent as their highest priority.

II. Listen to the conversation again and complete the following notes with what you hear.

1. Managerial talent refers to the people:
   — who can _____ ;
   — who can _____ ;
   — who can _____ ;
   — who can _____ .

2. Companies can enhance their performance:
   — by _____ ;
   — by _____ ;
   — by _____ .

3. In the keen talent competition, HR should take the role of:
   — _____ ;
   — _____ ;
   — _____ ;
   — _____ .

4. Affirmation is important to talent management as it:
   — makes people feel _____ ;
   — helps drive _____ .

Passage

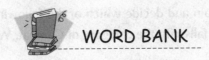

WORD BANK

wizard	/ˈwɪzəd/	*n.*	奇才
bribe	/braɪb/	*v.*	贿赂，向……行贿
strand	/strænd/	*v.*	使陷于困境
impede	/ɪmˈpiːd/	*v.*	阻止
proprietary	/prəˈpraɪətərɪ/	*a.*	私人拥有的
sabotage	/ˈsæbətɑːʒ/	*v.*	破坏
withhold	/wɪðˈhəʊld/	*v.*	保留
ideology	/ˌaɪdɪˈɒlədʒɪ/	*n.*	观念，思想方式

I. Listen to the passage and choose the best answers to the questions you hear.

1. A. To surpass one's rivals.　　　　B. To do better than one's competitors.

   C. To outdo what other people have done.　D. All of the above.

2. A. Physical violence.

   B. Winning at the cost of other people.

   C. Competing with one's rivals on an equal footing.

   D. Competing to be the strongest.

3. A. In the presence of sportsmanship.　B. In the nature of marketing methods.

   C. In the business ideology.　　　　D. In the scope of business.

4. A. It affects interpersonal relationship.

   B. It threatens the life of rivals.

   C. It denies people access to society's resources.

   D. It leads to one price war after another.

5. A. It is hard to tell the difference between combat and competition.

   B. It is hard to restrain oneself not to get involved in combat.

   C. It is hard to make a law and enforce it.

   D. It is hard for governments to do away with any form of combat.

II. Listen to the passage again and decide which of the following falls into the category of Competition and which falls into the category of Combat. Write A for Competition and B for Combat.

1. (   ) Enable the computer to perform more functions
2. (   ) Write the shortest working instructions for the computer
3. (   ) Claim one's copyright to a software package
4. (   ) Set up a new world record
5. (   ) Make a competitor lose by bribery
6. (   ) Let the best person win
7. (   ) Let me win, best or not
8. (   ) Compete by improving business operations
9. (   ) Compete by sabotaging the rival
10. (   ) Keep back information in order to keep the lead

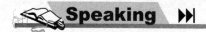 **Speaking** ▶▶

Discussion

☎ **Work in groups. Study the following case carefully and discuss what measures Mr. Williams could take to survive in the intense market competition.**

Mr. Williams is an instant noodle manufacturer. He has been in business for ten years. He did fairly well for the first four years. But with more people coming into the picture and more products in the market, his company is beginning to show signs of failure. Its market share has decreased from 17% to 9%. And it is also losing key employees to its major competitors. What is worse, the price it charges allows no room for further reduction. Mr. Williams is very worried. He knows if the process is not checked, his business will disappear from the market sooner or later.

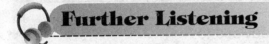

☎ **Work as a class. Compare and share your insights with the rest of the class.**

Further Listening

Short Recordings

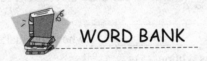

WORD BANK

posh	/pɒʃ/	*a.*	豪华的，奢侈的
code	/kəʊd/	*n.*	规范，惯例
primary	/ˈpraɪmərɪ/	*a.*	主要的，首要的
constructive	/kənˈstrʌktɪv/	*a.*	建设性的，积极的
abbreviation	/əˌbriːvɪˈeɪʃ(ə)n/	*n.*	缩写词，略语
dash	/dæʃ/	*n.*	破折号
punctuation	/ˌpʌŋktjuˈeɪʃ(ə)n/	*n.*	标点符号
dress up			盛装，打扮

I. **In this section, you will hear five short recordings. For each piece, decide what each speaker is giving advice about.**

Item 1. ....

Item 2. ....

Item 3. ....

Item 4. ....

Item 5. ....

A. writing letters

B. making telephone calls

C. writing a report

D. making notes

E. giving a presentation

F. entertaining visitors

G. arranging a conference

H. going for an interview

II. Listen to the five recordings again and complete the notes with what you hear.

While entertaining visitors, you are advised to:
✎ find out in advance (1) _____ .

While going for an interview, you are advised to:
✎ wear a suit unless you are absolutely sure that (2) _____ .

✎ allow yourself plenty of time to get there and have a few minutes to (3) _____

_____ .

✎ (4) _____ when you shake hands.

✎ answer the questions without (5) _____ .

✎ speak slowly.

While making telephone calls, you are advised to:
✎ make sure (6) _____ .

✎ let them know in advance you're calling so that (7) _____ .

✎ speak slowly and clearly.

✎ confirm (8) _____ .

✎ not pretend you've understood them if you haven't.

While writing a report, you are advised to:
✎ think about (9) _____ first.

✎ think about (10) _____ and leave the

(11) _____ until later.

✎ check the (12) _____ and write the (13) _____ .

✎ (14) _____ when the report is complete.

While making notes, you are advised to:
✎ (15) _____ whenever you can, but not so many that you can't

understand them later.

✎ put in words like (16) _____ as they can show how

your ideas are related.

✎ (17) _____ so you can expand them later if you need to.

✎ (18) _____ as it's a very useful punctuation mark.

Home Listening

Business News

WORD BANK

Oxfam	一家世界援助组织
Matagalpa	美它加尔帕（尼加拉瓜咖啡盛产地）
Nicaragua	尼加拉瓜（拉丁美洲国家）

Listen to the business news report and choose the best answers to the questions you hear.

1. A. They have dropped by almost fifteen percent over the last three years.

   B. They have dropped by almost fifteen percent over the last thirty years.

   C. They have dropped by almost fifty percent over the last three years.

   D. They have dropped by almost fifty percent over the last thirty years.

2. A. Because the world coffee production has grown greatly.

   B. Because the world coffee market is dwindling quickly.

   C. Because tea and fruit juice, instead of coffee, are becoming popular.

   D. Because it requires more investment than before in coffee growing.

3. A. The introduction of man-made chemical fertilizers.

   B. More productive kinds of coffee plants.

   C. A better price of coffee sold on the world market.

   D. Both a and b.

4. A. More agreeable weather.

B. Technology-enriched growing methods.

C. Growing coffee plants under fruit trees.

D. More investment in production methods.

5. A. Corporate coffee producers.　　　　B. Minor coffee producers.

C. "Fair trade coffee" producers.　　　　D. Farmers using traditional methods.

Unit 12

● **Business Ethics**

Dictation

• •

Listen to the following short paragraph and fill in the blanks with what you hear.

Ethical questions range from practical, narrowly defined issues, such as a company's (1) _____, to broader social and philosophical questions, such as a company's (2) _____ _____ and (3) _____.

Many ethical conflicts develop from conflicts between the differing interests of company owners and (4) _____. Managers must balance the ideal against the practical — the need to (5) _____ _____ with honesty in business practices, (6) _____ _____, and larger environmental and social issues.

Ethical issues in business have become more complicated because of (7) _____ _____ and because of (8) _____ _____ that define the limits of criminal behavior.

Listening & Speaking

SECTION A   **Ethical Principles**

Pre-listening ▶▶

Discussion

Discuss the following questions with your partner and take notes when necessary.

1. Do you know any business scandals and what lessons can we learn from them?

——

——

2. Do you think it pays to adhere to high corporate ethical standards in the face of ruthless business competition?

——

——

Listening ▶▶

Conversation

WORD BANK

ethics	/ˈeθɪks/	*n.*	道德规范

integrate	/'ıntıgreıt/	*v.*	使……并入
implement	/'ımplımənt/	*v.*	执行
initiative	/ı'nıʃıətıv/	*n.*	主动性，积极性
deliberation	/dı,lıbə'reıʃ(ə)n/	*n.*	熟思，考虑
discipline	/'dısıplın/	*n.*	学科；纪律
submission	/səb'mıʃən/	*n.*	提交，呈递
roll out			铺开，开展

I. Listen to the conversation and decide whether the following statements are true or false. Write T for true and F for false in the brackets.

1. (　) Globalization tends to complicate the ethical issues in the world of business.

2. (　) To maximize profits, multinational corporations choose to operate in countries where lack of concern for the environment is neither illegal nor unethical.

3. (　) Corporations that have overseas operations are suggested to compromise between their ethical standards and the local rules.

4. (　) The knowledge and skills of business ethics are highly appreciated by employers as the costs of corporate crime can be high.

5. (　) Courses are provided at some colleges of commerce to prepare students with skills and expertise needed in the field of business ethics.

6. (　) It usually takes as long as a few months to plan, develop, and roll out a specific business ethics program for a company.

7. (　) The cost of a business ethics program usually depends on how comprehensive the initiative is and how big the business is.

8. (　) Not all organizations or societies are providing ethics-related guidance and assistance for profit.

9. (　) Short and occasional training sessions are more recommendable for small businesses as it is not worthwhile for them to implement a business ethics program.

10. (　) High standards of corporate practice can't be guaranteed unless corporations are continually dedicated to improving its overall ethics initiative.

II. Listen to the conversation again and complete the notes with what you hear.

Resources Available	Ways to Promote Business Ethics
Colleges of Commerce & Graduate School of Business	📁 Integrating (1) _____ as an opportunity to (2) _____ that provides the skills and expertise needed. 📁 Providing an opportunity for (3) _____ _____.
Societies & Organizations	*For companies:* 📁 Providing (4) _____ to those that seek guidance and assistance with (5) _____ _____ within the corporate context. *For individuals:* 📁 Organizing and offering (6) _____ _____. 📁 Providing (7) _____.
Internet	📁 Providing diverse online resources, such as online library, online News Room, etc. to (8) _____.
Publications	📁 Publishing (9) _____ on all aspects of business ethics. 📁 Encouraging articles from disciplines such as (10) _____ _____. 📁 Accepting submissions of relevant writings from individual readers.

Passage

WORD BANK

transgression	/træns'greʃən/	*n.*	违反；犯罪
circulate	/'sɜːkjuleɪt/	*v.*	（使）流通，（使）传播

incongruity	/ˌɪnkɔŋ'gruːɪtɪ/	*n.*	不协调，不适宜
suffice	/sə'faɪs/	*v.*	足够；有能力
organ	/'ɔ:gən/	*n.*	机关报；机构

1. Listen to the passage and choose the best answers to the questions you hear.

1. A. Ethics are as important as many other things.

   B. Ethics are not important at all.

   C. Ethics are less important than many other things.

   D. Whether ethics are truly important is unknown.

2. A. Clarify mission statement on corporate values.

   B. Set up code of conduct.

   C. Do some analysis and identify problems.

   D. Get code of conduct（行动守则）circulated.

3. A. Surveys.　　　　B. Questionnaires.　　　　C. Interviews.　　　　D. Seminars.

4. A. The company has respect for its employees.

   B. The company does not respect its employees.

   C. The employees are meddlesome（爱管闲事的）.

   D. The boss is imperious（专横的）.

5. A. On the company's wired TV.　　　　　　B. Via the company's intercom.

   C. In the company's house organ.　　　　　　D. At the staff meeting.

II. Listen to the passage again and decide whether the following statements are true or false. Write T for true and F for false in the brackets.

1. (　　) Companies usually give corporate ethics high priority, but many employees care little about it.

2. (　　) A company should be "mad" about ethical transgressions, so its employees will get the message that the management does care about them.

3. (　　) The vast majority of the Fortune 1000 companies have clarified a statement on their corporate values.

4. (　　) More must be done to strengthen corporate ethical commitment than simply introduce and circulate codes of conduct.

5. (　　) Over 90 percent of the Fortune 1000 companies have brought out their codes of conduct, and some of them even go further to circulate these codes of conduct.

6. (   ) At a company that has respect for its employees the boss usually listens to the employees and seeks for their opinions.

7. (   ) It is advisable for companies to encourage employee participation in identifying inconsistencies between its words and its actions.

8. (   ) Cash payment is the most welcome reward to employees who help to identify company ethical problems.

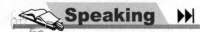 **Speaking** ▶▶

Story-telling

☎ **Work in groups. Study and discuss the picture with the help of the following questions.**

❏ How do you understand the relationship between the two men?
❏ Where are the two men?
❏ What are the two men doing?
❏ What does one man show to the other?
❏ Why does the man say that?

☎ **Work in groups. Make up a story according to what you read from the picture. Try to make your story as dramatic as possible.**

☎ **Work as a class. Share your story with your classmates. Select your favorite one and explain why you love it most.**

How close to the truth do you want to come, sir?

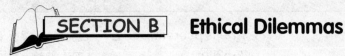

SECTION B   **Ethical Dilemmas**

Pre-listening ▶▶▶

Discussion

Discuss the following questions with your partner and take notes when necessary.

1. What ethical dilemmas do people in business often experience?

----

2. How can companies encourage good business ethics in their employees?

Listening ▶▶

Conversation

WORD BANK

fraud	/frɔːd/	*n.*	欺骗，欺诈行为
rigid	/ˈrɪdʒɪd/	*a.*	严格的

transparent	/træns'pɛərənt/	*a.*	透明的；显然的
undue	/ˌʌn'djuː/	*a.*	不适当的
component	/kəm'pəunənt/	*n.*	组成部分，成分
fraudulent	/'frɔdjulənt/	*a.*	欺骗性的，欺诈性的
vendor	/'vendə(r)/	*n.*	卖主
certified public accountant			注册会计师
orientation program			新员工培训项目

I. Listen to the conversation and choose the best answers to the questions you hear.

1. A. Ask candidates to submit a copy of detailed resume.

   B. Have a thorough background investigation.

   C. Test candidates' integrity via questionnaires.

   D. Interview the people around the candidates.

2. A. He sets goals solely.

   B. He exerts pressure on employees to bring out hard work.

   C. He makes friends with his employees.

   D. He sets goals and offers help to achieve the goals.

3. A. Clarify fraudulent behaviors as well as their implications.

   B. Announce the result of the new employees' background investigation.

   C. Set work goals in a professional way.

   D. Familiarize new recruits with corporation rules.

4. A. Spend the money quickly.   B. Collect the money secretly.

   C. Notify the cashier.   D. Blame the cashier.

5. A. A loose corporate culture.   B. Heavy workload.

   C. Unprofessional operation.   D. All of the above.

6. A. Frauds will never occur in a rigid corporate culture.

   B. Taking gifts from vendors is allowed in many companies.

   C. Frauds take place in different forms.

   D. Ethical employees will never do the wrong thing.

II. Listen to the conversation again and complete the notes with what you hear.

How to Build a Fraud-free Culture

Fraud is more likely to take place in a corporate culture where management has:

📁 (1) _____.

📁 (2) _____.

To keep potential frauds from joining top management, companies should conduct a thorough background investigation, i.e.:

📁 to (3) _____.

📁 to (4) _____.

To reduce the temptation to commit fraud, managers are advised:

📁 to (5) _____.

📁 to communicate the set goals.

📁 to (6) _____.

📁 to (7) _____.

📁 not to (8) _____.

📁 not to (9) _____.

Other things can be done to build a fraud-free culture:

📁 to include a component on fraud in (10) _____.

📁 to operate in a very professional way.

Passage

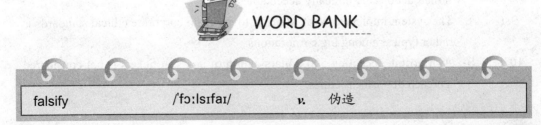

WORD BANK

| falsify | /ˈfɔːlsɪfaɪ/ | v. | 伪造 |

tally	/ˈtælɪ/	v.	计算；记录
breach	/briːtʃ/	n.	破坏，破裂
intact	/ɪnˈtækt/	a.	完整无缺的
anonymous	/əˈnɒnɪməs/	a.	匿名的
avenue	/ˈævɪnjuː/	n.	方法，途径
Enron			安然公司（全美最大的能源交易商，因财务丑闻于 2001 年 12 月 2 日宣布申请破产）
Marriot International			万豪酒店集团

I. Listen to the passage and decide whether the following statements are true or false. Write T for true and F for false in the brackets.

1. (   ) It is quite justifiable to falsify records if it benefits all the parties involved.

2. (   ) Compared with what officials at Enron did, the act of accepting gifts from clients is not unethical at all.

3. (   ) If we give little regard to our daily actions, we may end up with larger breaches in business ethics.

4. (   ) Policies and codes are formulated at many large organizations to ensure the intactness of their organizational values.

5. (   ) Marriott's "integrity test" is a list of questions designed to test employers' personality and competence.

6. (   ) Only candidates who passed the "integrity self-test" would be recruited at Marriott International.

7. (   ) Employees who report unethical behaviors are required to leave their contact information at Marriott's business integrity department for further investigation.

8. (   ) Employees at Marriott can consult the business-integrity department to check if their actions are ethically acceptable or not.

9. (   ) The system implemented at Marriott to maintain corporate ethical standards is rather typical among big corporations.

10. (   ) At Marriott, accepting 500 dollars' worth of box seat tickets is not considered a breach of business ethics.

II. Listen to the passage again and complete the notes with what you hear.

Ethical or Not Ethical?

Common daily ethical dilemmas:

✎ Is it OK to (1) _____?

✎ Is it OK to take the gift a client sent you when your immediate superior tells you
to do so, despite (2) _____?

✎ Is it OK to (3) _____
when they play "teacher"?

Questions included on the Marriott Integrity self-test:

✎ (4) _____?

✎ How would you feel after (5) _____?

✎ (6) _____?

✎ What would you do if (7) _____ and (8) _____
_____?

Speaking ▶▶

Discussion & Case study

☎ Work in groups. Study the following two business ethics cases and decide how you
would manage each situation. You may find the following three-step process for
solving an ethical problem useful.

Step 1: Analyze the consequences.
   📁 Who will be helped by what you do?
   📁 Who will be harmed?

◻ What kind of benefits and harms are we talking about?

◻ How does all of this look over the long run as well as the short run?

Step 2: Analyze the actions. Consider all of the options from a different perspective, without thinking about the consequences.

◻ How do the actions measure up against moral principles like honesty, fairness, equality, respecting the dignity of others, and people's rights? Consider the common good.

◻ Does any of the actions "cross the line"?

◻ If there's a conflict between principles or between the rights of different people involved, is there a way to see one principle as more important than the others?

◻ Which option offers actions that are least problematic?

Step 3: Make a decision. Take both parts of your analysis into account and make a decision.

☎ **Work as class. Announce your decisions to your classmates, and justify them as well. Note that these dilemmas come to you without their real-life resolutions. You are encouraged to think for yourself about how you might resolve them, since the nature of each dilemma is highly individualistic.**

Case Study 1 — Integrity in Business

You are a recruiter for an executive recruitment firm that has recently been retained by one of the largest corporations in the United States to find appropriate candidates for the position of President of the corporation. If the corporation hires one of the candidates you find then your firm will receive one third of the President's cash compensation — salary and bonus, an amount in excess of $750,000. Several weeks into the recruitment process it becomes clear to you that the company has gone about the search in a severely flawed way, making it highly unlikely that it will find the kind of candidates it needs. The Board of Directors, in your judgment, has allowed the CEO to control the search. It is clear to you that he wants someone who will be deferential towards him, which, in your judgment, will make it extremely difficult to attract the most highly qualified candidates. You discuss the issue with your superior. She says that given the intensely competitive environment for executive search firms, it would seriously disadvantage your firm to offend the Board of Directors of one of America's largest corporations. She reminds you that the Board of Directors is responsible for hiring the President of the Corporation. A recruitment firm, she says, bears no legal liability if a candidate it presents to a company is hired and proves unsuccessful in his position.

What should you do in this situation, and why?

Case Study 2 — Market or "Friend" Rental Rate?

You approve leases for Rayside Properties, a real-estate company. One day, Elaine, a real-estate appraiser, approached you to inquire about leasing office space in one of the company's buildings. Elaine had previously rented space in a Rayside's building, but that building had been sold and Elaine had to find new space at the end of her lease. You would like to rent to Elaine — she is not only an ideal tenant with an excellent credit record with the company, but also you know that Elaine is in the position to speak favorably to others about your company's good service and careful maintenance of their buildings. In addition, Elaine is a close family friend. You have the perfect space for Elaine coming available just when she needs it. The problem is, rental rates have increased quite a bit since Elaine signed her last lease with Rayside, and it is more than she wants to pay. Elaine asks you for a break on the rent.

What should you do in this situation, and why?

Further Listening

Short Recordings

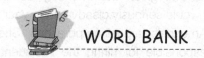
WORD BANK

trip	/ trɪp /	v.	绊倒，摔倒
bump	/'bʌmp/	v.	碰撞
workshop	/'wəːkʃɔp/	n.	专题研讨会
presentation	/ˌprezən'teɪʃ(ə)n/	n.	陈述，表达，发言
gadget	/'gædʒɪt/	n.	小器具，小配件
collate	/kə'leɪt/	v.	整理，核对
nightmare	/'naɪtmeə(r)/	n.	恶梦，可怕的事物
work station			工作区，工作站
core time			核心时间

I. In this section, you will hear five short recordings. For each piece, decide what each speaker is giving advice about.

Item 1. ....

Item 2. ....

Item 3. ....

Item 4. ....

Item 5. ....

A. product design

B. office furniture

C. staff development

D. overtime

E. shift patterns

F. interviews

G. flextime

H. presentations

II. Listen to the five recordings again and choose the best answers to the questions you hear.

1. A. The staff receive a higher rate if they work extra hours during the week.

   B. The staff receive no overtime pay if they work extra hours during the week.

   C. The staff receive a double pay rate if they work on weekends.

   D. The staff receive a higher pay rate if they work on weekends.

2. A. You may leave the employer the impression that you are reliable.

   B. You may have time to calm yourself and check your appearance.

   C. You may avoid bumping into the office furniture in a hurry.

   D. You may give yourself plenty of time to imagine what to say.

3. A. All-round training.   B. Advanced training.

   C. Personalized training.   D. Technical training.

4. A. Expanding office space.   B. Purchasing electronic gadgets.

   C. Updating technology system.   D. Redesigning work stations.

5. A. The time when all employees in the office must meet a deadline.

   B. The time when some employees are allowed to stagger work hours.

   C. The time when all employees must be at their place of employment.

   D. The time when some employees can choose to work at home.

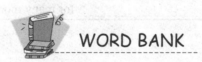

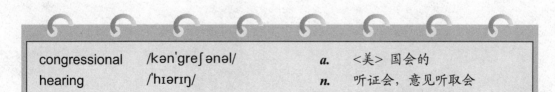

WORD BANK

| congressional | /kənˈɡreʃənəl/ | *a.* | <美> 国会的 |
| hearing | /ˈhɪərɪŋ/ | *n.* | 听证会，意见听取会 |

| Justice Department | （美国）司法部 |
| Labor Department | （美国）劳工部 |

Listen to the business news report and complete the notes with what you hear.

<table>
<tr><td colspan="2" align="center">The Failure of Enron</td></tr>
<tr>
<td>Enron's Background</td>
<td>Enron, one of the largest companies in the United States, is an (1) _____ _____, with headquarters situated in (2) _____ _____, Texas.</td>
</tr>
<tr>
<td>Financial Conditions</td>
<td>Unable to pay the thousands of millions of dollars of debts, Enron has asked a federal court for (3) _____. As a result, the value of Enron stock quickly fell and closed Thursday at (4) _____ _____, while each share of Enron stock sold for (5) _____ _____ less than a year ago.</td>
</tr>
<tr>
<td>Influence on Employees</td>
<td>Enron has already dismissed (6) _____ of its more than (7) _____ workers.
Besides loss of jobs, Enron employees lost the money they invested in the company as part of their (8) _____, which had already lost more than (9) _____.</td>
</tr>
<tr>
<td>Influence on Market</td>
<td>Enron's failure is affecting (10) _____ in many countries including (11) _____, (12) _____ and (13) _____.
Experts predict a loss of at least (14) _____ for companies and banks that have lent money to Enron.</td>
</tr>
<tr>
<td>Cause of Failure</td>
<td>The cause of Enron's failure will be the subject of (15) _____ _____ for many months to come.</td>
</tr>
</table>

Unit 13

Negotiation

Preliminary Listening

Dictation

Listen to the following short paragraph and fill in the blanks with what you hear.

Negotiation is the process of two individuals or groups (1) _____
_____. It applies knowledge from the fields of
(2) _____. Whenever an
economic transaction takes place or (3) _____, negotiation occurs; for
example, when (4) _____ or businesses negotiate salaries with
employees. The (5) _____ can vary based
on cultural differences. In international negotiations, obstacles arise when negotiating
teams possess (6) _____.
Negotiators often assume that shared beliefs exist when, in reality, they do not. These
cultural factors affect (7) _____, negotiating strategies,
(8) _____, emotional aspects,
decision making and contractual and administrative elements.

Listening & Speaking

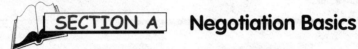

SECTION A **Negotiation Basics**

Pre-listening ▶▶|

Discussion

Discuss the following questions with your partner and take notes when necessary.

1. Describe a situation in your life in which you had to negotiate with somebody, say, a family member, a friend, or a work associate. How do you like the outcome of the negotiation?

   ----

2. The following expressions are often used to describe the negotiation outcomes. Explain how you understand them by using an analogy.
   - ❑ LOSE/LOSE
   - ❑ WIN/LOSE
   - ❑ DRAW
   - ❑ WIN/WIN

Listening ▶▶|

Conversation

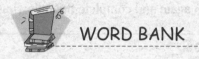

WORD BANK

title	/ˈtaɪtl/	*n.*	书目，已出版或即将出版的书面作品
quote	/kwəut/	*n.*	报价
commitment	/kəˈmɪtmənt/	*n.*	承诺，委托事项
testimonial	/ˌtestɪˈməunɪəl/	*n.*	（品格、行为、资格等的）证明书，推荐书
reference	/ˈrefərəns/	*n.*	推荐信，证明
credit	/ˈkredɪt/	*v.*	存入（账户），记入贷方
incentive	/ɪnˈsentɪv/	*n.*	刺激，鼓励

I. Listen to the conversation and choose the best answers to the questions you hear.

1. A. A suitable color bubble jet printer.
   B. A series of high-quality color art books.
   C. A printing company for their next series.
   D. A renowned 21ˢᵗ century woman painter.

2. A. A British company.
   B. An Italian company.
   C. A Hong Kong-based company.
   D. A San Francisco-based company.

3. A. Because it charges for delivery on the first title.
   B. Because it cannot present any reliable references.
   C. Because it is only interested in printing all ten titles.
   D. Because it is located far away from Bright Publications.

4. A. Because it insists on charging for delivery.
   B. Because it refuses to make any concession on price.
   C. Because he is not assured of the quality of its work.
   D. Because he has not got his boss's permission to do so.

5. A. It is the first time that Bright Publications will cooperate with Conti.
   B. Delivery charge is the first consideration for Bright Publications.
   C. Conti offers Tony Davis a 5 per cent commission to obtain the contract.
   D. Bright Publications will get the contract signed by the end of next week.

II. Listen to the conversation again and complete the following chart with what you hear.

The Preparation Phase

This is where you work out what you want and which is your priority.

Bright Publications cares most about (1)
(tick the correct option)

☐ price

☐ quality

☐ printer's location

The Debating Phase

You try to find out what the other side wants. Say what you want, but do not say what your final conditions are. Try to find out in what areas the other side may be prepared to move.

Yip obviously wants to get the contract of (2) _____
_____.

Tony gets the message that (3) _____ and (4) _____
are the areas where Yip can make some compromise.

The Proposal Phase

This is the point at which you suggest some of the things you could trade. Be patient and listen to the other side's proposals.

If the printing job for the first title is satisfactory, Tony can give (5) _____
_____ based on the condition that Conti (6) _____
_____.

When Yip offers to sign the contract right away, Tony says he will contact
her next week because (7) _____.

The Bargaining Phase

This is the part where you indicate what it is you will actually trade.

Yip prompts Tony to sign the agreement as early as possible by (8) _____
_____.

Passage

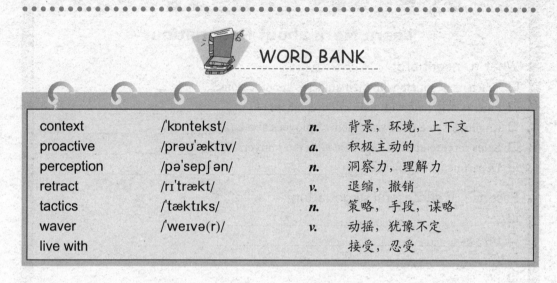

WORD BANK

context	/ˈkɒntekst/	*n.*	背景，环境，上下文
proactive	/prəʊˈæktɪv/	*a.*	积极主动的
perception	/pəˈsepʃən/	*n.*	洞察力，理解力
retract	/rɪˈtrækt/	*v.*	退缩，撤销
tactics	/ˈtæktɪks/	*n.*	策略，手段，谋略
waver	/ˈweɪvə(r)/	*v.*	动摇，犹豫不定
live with			接受，忍受

I. Listen to the passage and complete the chart with what you hear.

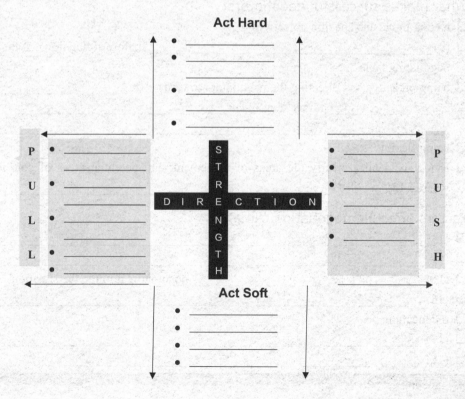

II. Listen to the passage again and complete the notes with what you hear.

Learn More about Negotiation

What to negotiate:
- ❑ Teachers negotiate with their students about lessons.
- ❑ Parents negotiate with their children about (1) _____.
- ❑ Employers negotiate with their employees about (2) _____.
- ❑ Sales representatives negotiate with their buyers on (3) _____.
- ❑ Departments negotiate on (4) _____.

Essence of successful negotiation:
- ❑ (5) _____
- ❑ (6) _____
- ❑ (7) _____
- ❑ (8) _____

What makes successful negotiators:
- ❑ having broad and specific objectives
- ❑ (9) _____ before sitting down at the negotiating table
- ❑ being proactive and directing the negotiators towards (10) _____ rather than (11) _____
- ❑ being flexible
- ❑ trying to identify clearly the areas of agreement, and potential areas of conflict where (12) _____

Factors affecting negotiation climate:
- ❑ (13) _____
- ❑ (14) _____
- ❑ (15) _____ negotiators bring to the situation
- ❑ (16) _____
- ❑ the location
- ❑ (17) _____
- ❑ (18) _____

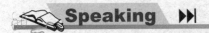

Speaking ▶▶|

Role-play & Discussion

☎ **Work in pairs. First you and your partner decide which role to play and then study each other's task sheet respectively.**

For student A

○
○ **ROLE A**
○
○
○
○ Company Profile
○
○ Occupation: Managing Director
○ Company: Sunrays Inc., manufacturer of sportswear and sports equipment
○ Performance: In the 1990s Sunrays was a world-famous name and 4 world champions
○   used its equipment; Sales are low and Sunrays badly needs new
○   marketing ideas
○ Strategy: To persuade the world's newest tennis star to promote your products
○
○
○ Negotiating Brief
○
○ **You can offer**
○ ● $12 million over 5 years
○ ● free equipment and good practice facilities
○ ● publicity
○ ● the chance of a career with the company when the player retires
○
○ **You want**
○ ● exclusive rights for 5 years: to use only Sunrays equipment and clothing
○ ● 30 days a year of the player's time for promotional work: photographs, exhibition,
○   games, interviews and testing of equipment
○ ● to choose an agent to protect the player's "image" (to manage press interviews and
○   generally to look after him)

For student B

ROLE B

Personal Profile

Occupation: Tennis player, ranked No. 15 in the world (playing professionally for 26 months)

Age: 19 years old

Interests: Playing tennis; traveling; spending time privately

Negotiating Brief

You can offer

- Excellent publicity (you expect to be one of the top five players in the world next year)

- 1 day a month for photographs, interviews or exhibition (possibly 2 days in the winter months)

You want

- good practice facilities

- to continue to use the racquet you use at the moment (not a Sunrays)

- a percentage of sales (for products which carry your name)

- a two-year contract (not longer)

- some free time to yourself

☎ Work in groups. Two or three pairs work together as a group. Each pair acts out the negotiation in turn, with the rest watching over their performance.

☎ Work in groups. Comment on each other's performance in the course of negotiation and discuss how you can improve your negotiation skills, strategies and outcomes.

 SECTION B   **Negotiation Styles**

Pre-listening ▶▶

Discussion

· ·

Discuss the following questions with your partner and take notes when necessary.

1. Negotiation often arises out of conflict. What can you do, as a negotiator, to reduce the atmosphere of conflict in negotiation?

----

2. Suppose you will be negotiating in a foreign language. As a non-native speaker of the language, what advantages and disadvantages do you have in the process of negotiation?

Listening ▶▶

Conversation

· ·

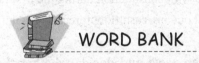 WORD BANK

envisage	/ɪnˈvɪzɪdʒ/	*v.*	设想，预见
launch	/lɔːntʃ/	*n.*	新产品投放市场
nominal	/ˈnɒmmɪnəl/	*a.*	极少的，微不足道的
consultation	/ˌkɒnsəlˈteɪʃən/	*n.*	磋商，咨询

do one's homework	做充分的准备工作
write off	取消，注销
a token fee	象征性收费
in the interest(s) of	为了，为……的利益

I. Listen to the conversation and choose the best answers to the questions you hear.

1. A. Patent transfer.   B. Collaboration scope.
   C. Production capacity.   D. Investment volume.

2. A. One in the States and one in China, both having an annual capacity of 30,000 VC10 units and 2,000 HB2 units.
   B. One in China and one in Europe, both having an annual capacity of 3,000 VC10 units and 2,000 HB2 units.
   C. One in Europe and one in China, both having an annual capacity of 3,000 VC10 units and 20,000 HB2 units.
   D. One in China and one in Japan, both having an annual capacity of 30,000 VC10 units and 20,000 HB2 units.

3. A. 14 millions.   B. 17 millions.   C. 40 millions.   D. 57 millions.

4. A. By keeping all the R&D work within Teltron.
   B. By providing full consultation for the joint venture.
   C. By charging the joint venture a nominal license fee.
   D. By writing off Hi-Cam's investment in the R&D work.

5. A. Teltron will charge a license fee to the joint venture for its basic inventions.
   B. Teltron maintains that both the R&D work and patents remain in Teltron.
   C. Teltron only guarantees full consultation during the first phase of the project.
   D. Teltron has not carried out any cash flow forecasts for the joint venture project.

II. Listen to the conversation again and decide whether the following statements are true or false. Write T for true and F for false in the brackets.

1. (   ) Mr. Young, the CEO of Hi-Cam visits Teltron's head office in person to negotiate their joint venture.

2. (   ) Hi-Cam and Teltron have held an exploratory session of negotiation earlier that morning.

3. (　　) For that morning's negotiation, Hi-Cam expects to define the scope of the joint venture.

4. (　　) Mr. Young's position is that both of the two production centers should be located in China.

5. (　　) The investment figures put forward by Teltron include the expenses of introducing the products to the market.

6. (　　) Mr. Hamilton is optimistic about the prospect of the joint venture for their VC10 and HB2 products.

7. (　　) Teltron will hold the basic patents because Hi-Cam contributes nothing to the further R&D work.

8. (　　) Teltron will charge Hi-Cam a nominal license fee in compensation for Hi-Cam's investment in R&D.

9. (　　) Teltron insists that both the R&D work and patents should remain in the Teltron parent company.

10. (　　) The negotiation between Teltron and Hi-Cam came to a deadlock over the R&D expenditure and patents.

Passage

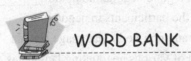

WORD BANK

actor	/ˈæktə(r)/	*n.*	参与者
long-standing	/ˌlɒŋˈstædɪŋ/	*a.*	长期的，长久的
exploit	/ɪkˈsplɔɪt/	*v.*	利用
blend	/blend/	*n.*	混合，混合物
linguistic	/lɪŋˈgwɪstɪk/	*a.*	语言（学）的
one-off	/ˈwʌnɒf/	*a.*	一次性的

I. Listen to the passage and choose the best answers to complete the following statements.

1. In a cooperative style of negotiation, _____.
   A. both sides will exploit every possibility to get the best result from the negotiation
   B. both sides will show a willingness to lose something for the sake of mutual friendship and cooperation
   C. both sides will benefit more in the long run in friendship and cooperation even if they make some concessions
   D. both sides will try to understand each other's needs and to develop strategies to maintain long-standing relationship

2. In a competitive style of negotiation, _____.
   A. neither party will consider future cooperation with each other
   B. neither party will show satisfaction at the outcome of the negotiation
   C. both parties will resort to hostile and threatening language and gestures
   D. both parties will take advantage of each other's weaknesses to gain the most

3. In negotiating, it is advisable to _____.
   A. treat the actors in negotiation and the issue under negotiation in indifferent ways
   B. schedule a meeting on a Friday evening to speed up the decision-making process
   C. use aggressive, hostile and threatening language, especially in competitive negotiating
   D. baffle your opponent by complicating the task with indirect and impersonal forms of language

4. According to the passage, a good negotiator should _____.
   A. be on rapport with all the participants in negotiating
   B. be alert to both verbal and non-verbal language signals
   C. have a good command of various negotiating languages
   D. try to seek a solution satisfactory to both negotiating sides

5. It cannot be concluded from the passage that _____.
   A. human factors add complexity to the process of negotiation
   B. most negotiations embrace both competition and cooperation
   C. cooperative style negotiations bring about the win-win outcome
   D. competitive style negotiations dominate today's business world

II. Listen to the passage again and answer the following questions briefly with what you hear.

1. What are the facts that negotiators must be aware of?

_____

_____

2. What will influence the strategy to be adopted in negotiating?

_____

3. What personal needs of the actors in negotiating must be taken into account?

_____

_____

4. What do researchers who have studied the negotiating process recommend?

_____

_____

5. What is responsible for the sometimes complex style of negotiating language?

_____

_____

6. When is the cooperative style of negotiation likely to take place?

_____

_____

7. In what case is it appropriate to use the competitive style of negotiation?

_____

_____

8. What will skilled negotiators be sensitive to? And why?

_____

_____

Speaking ▶▶|

Case Study & Discussion

☎ Work in groups. Study the following case and discuss what explains the undesirable outcome of the negotiation meetings between the Americans and the Japanese.

Case Study

For a number of months, a large advertising company was discussing the possibility of buying a small Japanese company so as to have a foothold in the

Japanese market. The American CEO saw the merger as a positive one for both sides and thought the time was right to send over a negotiating team comprised of the company lawyer and his Vice-President for International Marketing to "close the deal".

The American negotiating team arrived in Tokyo on Sunday. They hoped they could come to terms by Wednesday or Friday at the latest. They wanted to get right down to detailed negotiations and didn't understand the daily invitations to lunch and dinner extended by their Japanese negotiating partners. They assumed dinner and drinks, once the negotiation had been successfully concluded, would be sufficient. By Thursday, they were still far apart on a final agreement. The Americans, frustrated with what they saw as lack of movement, told the Japanese negotiating team that they had to see some progress on major issues which they could take back with them when they left on Friday.

Even though both the Japanese and the Americans were genuinely interested in the merger, the talks failed to bring the two sides closer together. Both the Japanese and the Americans left the negotiations thinking the other side had been most unreasonable.

☎ **Work in groups. Different cultures approach negotiating in different ways. Discuss and compare the differences and similarities between traditional American and Chinese negotiation styles.**

American Negotiators	Chinese Negotiators
Negotiating is often seen as a competitive venture. Looking for the best deal often results in a win-lose orientation in which American negotiators strive to get the best short-term gains, sometimes overlooking or ignoring the benefits of a long-term relationship.	
Americans want to focus on the issues and get the job done in a short period of time. They want discussions that get to the point quickly. They may become impatient with long, drawn-out negotiations. Their style may be perceived as overly direct and even aggressive.	

continued

American Negotiators	Chinese Negotiators
Americans expect a degree of clarity, directness, and openness of intention at the bargaining table. "You tell me what you want, I'll tell you what I want and we'll proceed from there."	
Americans approach a complex negotiation by breaking down the issues that need to be addressed into a series of sub-issues or parts. They look to settle each part, one at a time, in a sequential or logical order.	
The American value of equality and informality in human relations results in a minimizing status differences around the conference table.	
American negotiators usually have the authority to make final commitments or agreements.	
Americans want to conclude the deal with a very precise written contract or agreement. Expect that contracts will be detailed and lengthy and shall be followed exactly as written by both parties.	
Generally, Americans don't expect to spend as much time discussing the overall framework or establishing the relationship between the parties.	
Americans tend to make concessions only reluctantly at first, saving their major concessions until the later parts of the negotiation session. They may use threats or warnings to generate some movement in the process.	

☎ **Work as a class. Share your insights with the rest of the class.**

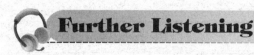
Further Listening

Short Recordings

WORD BANK

procurement	/prəˈkjʊəmənt/	n.	（政府的）收买，采购
stride	/straɪd/	n.	大步，阔步
rampant	/ˈræmpənt/	a.	猖獗的，猛烈的
piracy	/ˈpaɪərəsɪ/	n.	盗版，侵犯版权
trim	/trɪm/	v.	降低，减少
scale back			按比例逐步减少
refueling tanker			空中加油飞机
Pentagon			五角大楼（美国国防部）
Jackson			杰克逊（美国密西西比州首府）
Springdale			斯普林顿（美国阿肯色州西北部的一个城市）
Bellevue			贝尔维尤（位于华盛顿州的一个城市）

I. **In this section, you will hear five short recordings. For each piece, decide why each company decided to cut its workforce.**

1. AT&T Corp. ....

2. Boeing Co. ....

3. Tyson Foods Inc. ....

4. Warner Music ....

5. Vivendi Universal Games ....

A. Government supervision
B. Company acquisition
C. Company restructuring
D. Cost reduction
E. Recession of economy
F. Automation of facilities
G. Decrease in market demand
H. Suspension of an important deal

II. Listen to the five short recordings again and complete the table with what you hear.

Company	Workforce Cut Fact Sheet
AT&T Corp. *the nation's largest* (1) _____ _____	To cut 8 percent of AT&T workforce, or about (2) _____ jobs, leaving it with about (3) _____ employees, as encouraged by the saving of $800 million from (4) _____ _____ in 2003.
Boeing Co. *the No. 2* (5) _____ _____ *and No. 2 Pentagon* contractor	To fire as many as 150 workers due to (6) _____ _____, which has been repeatedly delayed, first over (7) _____ and later over (8) _____ related to Boeing's hiring of a former Air Force procurement official.
Tyson Foods Inc. *the nation's* (9) _____ _____	To cut about 900 jobs at its Jackson, Mississippi-based (10) _____ later this year — a step in the midst of reducing its work force by about 5 percent, or nearly 6,000 jobs.
Warner Music *Entertainment*	To lay off about 1,000 people to help Warner Music (11) __ _____ in a rapidly evolving marketplace as the industry faces (12) _____ and (13) _____ _____ from other forms of entertainment despite recent strides to make money from (14) _____ _____.
Vivendi Universal Games *Video games*	To dismiss 350 employees at its Bellevue Studios within two months, following the last month's (15) _____ _____ for the reason that (16) _____ _____.

Home Listening

Business News

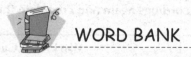

WORD BANK

plaintiff	/ˈpleɪntɪf/	n.	原告
gender	/ˈdʒendə(r)/	n.	性别
class action			共同起诉
NBC			美国国家广播公司（National Broadcasting Company）
Voice of America			美国之音（美国官方新闻机构，全球最大的新闻机构之一）

Listen to the business news report and decide whether the following statements are true or false. Write T for true and F for false in the brackets.

1. (   )   The federal court in the United States denied all the charges against Wal-Mart.

2. (   )   Wal-Mart is under the accusation of discriminating against women in respect of pay rise and promotion.

3. (   )   Wal-Mart case would be the largest sex-discrimination case against a public organization in the United States.

4. (   )   Susan Medolo, one of the plaintiffs, has worked at Wal-Mart over 15 years as a cashier.

5. (   )   Male managers are far better paid than female managers at Wal-Mart by reason that they are breadwinners of the family.

6. (   )   Wal-Mart refuses to admit the charges on the account that it takes hundreds of female managers into employment.

7. (   )   Stephanie Odle took a legal action against her employer when she was denied a pay rise she demanded.

8. (   )   The case has affected the performance of Wal-Mart share on the New York Stock Exchange because of worries about the lawsuit cost.

9. (   )   Wal-Mart shows great concern over the potential impact of the sex-bias case over its customers.

10. (   )   The Voice of America was found guilty of sex bias four years ago and had to pay 1,100 women $460,000 each.

Unit 14

Marketing

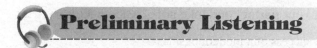
Dictation

Listen to the following short paragraph and fill in the blanks with what you hear.

The average consumer would probably define marketing as (1) _____ _____. It actually includes a good deal more. Modern marketing is most simply defined as activities that (2) _____ from producers to consumers. It encompasses, however, a broad range of activities including (3) _____ ... In advanced industrial economies, marketing considerations play a major role in determining corporate policy. Once primarily concerned with increasing sales through (4) _____, corporate marketing departments now focus on credit policies, product development, (5) _____ _____. Marketers may look for outlets through which to sell the company's products, including (6) _____ _____. Marketing is used both to (7) _____ _____ and to (8) _____.

Listening & Speaking

SECTION A **Marketing Mix**

Pre-listening ▶▶

Discussion

• •

Discuss the following questions with your partner and take notes when necessary.

1. What role does marketing play in the success of a modern business?

_____

_____

2. What do you think are the possible benefits and limitations of online marketing?

_____

_____

Listening ▶▶

Conversation

• •

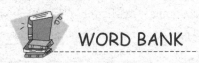

WORD BANK

scary	/ˈskeərɪ/	*a.*	引起惊慌的
affiliate	/əˈfɪlɪeɪt/	*n.*	附属机构，会员
sponsorship	/ˈspɒnsəʃɪp/	*n.*	赞助者的地位

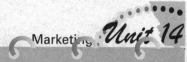

traffic	/ˈtræfɪk/	*n.*	一定时期内的顾客数量，流量
subscriber	/səbˈskraɪbə/	*n.*	用户，订户
jump into			参加，投入
pull in			吸收
sign up			签名，签约
team up			合作，协作
affiliate marketing			联属网络营销（独立的广告客户或网站所有者与商家达成协议，帮助其宣传产品或服务。这些联属机构通过促成销售赚取商家的佣金，付款和履约等事宜由商家处理）
Make A Living Online Member Site			由美国网络营销先驱 Jim Daniels 创建的一个网站，主要提供网络营销、网络创业方面的免费信息及相关咨询服务

I. Listen to the conversation and decide whether the following statements are true or false. Write T for true and F for false in the brackets.

1. (   ) Jim Daniels, a successful online marketer now, started his business with a very small budget.

2. (   ) It only takes Jim Daniels about half a year to generate a yearly income of six figures from his online business.

3. (   ) Jim Daniels was very confident of his success when he decided to quit his regular job and go full time online.

4. (   ) To Jim Daniels, making a living online means earning more while working less hours from the comfort of his own home.

5. (   ) According to Jim Daniels, owning a professional site of your own is a big key to long-term success online.

6. (   ) To ensure long-term success online, you should try your best to develop your own products and avoid affiliate programs.

7. (   ) Most of Jim Daniels' online income is attributable to his affiliate marketing programs.

8. (　　) If magazines that are read by a good percentage of the readership can't get traffic and make sales, there must be something wrong with their sales letter or site.

9. (　　) The pop-up script that Mark Caron used from Jim Daniels' *Make a Living Online Member Site* has doubled Mark's sign-up rate.

10. (　　) Cooperating with other publishers in the industry, you can increase your subscriber base by doing a cross-recommendation on the signup process.

II. Listen to the conversation again and complete the following notes with what you hear.

The Key to E-marketing Success

The road leading to achievement of marketing objectives:
- In Feb. 1996:　starting to (1) _____
- By May 1996:　starting to (2) _____
- By Nov. 1996:　starting to (3) _____
  _____ and deciding to go full time online

The elements bringing success to online-venture starters:
- (4) _____
  - ✓ the best road to take: (5) _____
  - ✓ in the meantime, (6) _____
- (7) _____

The way to start out with a limited budget:
- To find (8) _____
- To buy (9) _____

The sources of magazine subscribers:
- E-books
- Free reports
- (10) _____

Passage

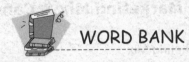

WORD BANK

variable	/'veərɪəbl/	*n.*	可变物，变量
intermediary	/ˌɪntə'miːdɪərɪ/	*n.*	中间人，媒介（物）
compatible	/kəm'pætəbl/	*a.*	谐调的，一致的
discounter	/'dɪskaʊntə/	*n.*	廉价零售店
attachment	/ə'tætʃmənt/	*n.*	附件，附加装置
built-in			内置的
in sum			总而言之，大体上

I. Listen to the passage and choose the best answers to the questions you hear.

1. A. What goods to sell. B. What packaging to use.
   C. What warranties to offer. D. What level of customer service to achieve.
2. A. Outlet locations. B. Supplier selections.
   C. Distribution channels. D. Transportation means.
3. A. Radio. B. Internet.
   C. Television. D. Newspaper.
4. A. Profit margin. B. Bundling strategy.
   C. Volume discounts. D. Advertising budget.
5. A. The sound marketing-mix concept contributes most to the business success of Cannon.

   B. Cannon usually applies several distinctive marketing mixes to one target market.

   C. Cannon mixes the four Ps to give a particular marketing mix for a particular market.

   D. Cannon attaches the same degrees of importance to the four Ps in different markets.

II. Listen to the passage again and complete the following notes with what you hear.

The Marketing Mix & Canon

What to Know about Marketing Mix

📂 The marketing mix is defined as a combination of marketing elements used to (1) ____
_____ and (2) _____.
📂 What marketing mixes to use is determined by (3) _____
and (4) _____.

Marketing Mixes Used by Canon

Target ╲ 4 Ps	For Beginners	For Serious Amateur Photographers
Product	offering (5) _____ _____ _____	offering (6) _____ _____ _____
Place	selling through (7) _____ _____	selling through (8) _____ _____
Price	retailing for (9) _____ _____	retailing for (10) _____ _____
Promotion	concentrating advertisement on (11) _____ _____	concentrating advertisement on (12) _____ _____
In conclusion	Canon markets (13) _____, promotes (14) _____, and has (15) _____.	

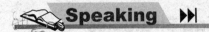

Speaking ▶▶|

Discussion

● ●

☎ **Work in groups. Discuss with your group and decide which P in the marketing mix is the key factor in marketing the following products or services. Explain why.**

- ❑ Fast food chain stores
- ❑ Sportswear products
- ❑ Household appliances
- ❑ Diary products
- ❑ Beauty & health products
- ❑ Insurance products
- ❑ Express delivery services
- ❑ Financial products

☎ **Work in groups. Discuss and work out the details of a marketing project on the basis of the following steps.**

Our Marketing Project

- ☐ What product or service to offer:

- ☐ How to inform customer of our new offering:

- ☐ How to price our product or service:

- ☐ How to distribute our product or service:

- ☐ What after-sales service to provide:

- ☐ Other things to consider:

☎ **Work as a class. Share your insights with the rest of the class.**

SECTION B Marketing Strategies

Pre-listening ▶▶

Discussion

· ·

Discuss the following questions with your partner and take notes when necessary.

1. What do you think is the key to marketing success in today's business world?

----

2. Do you know any unsuccessful marketing case(s)? And what do you think is responsible for the marketing failure(s)?

Listening ▶▶

Conversation

· ·

WORD BANK

| marketer | /'mɑːkɪtə(r)/ | n. | 营销人员，在市场上做买卖的人 |
| function | /'fʌŋkʃən/ | n. | 功能，职务，职责 |

portfolio	/ˌpɔːtˈfəʊlɪəʊ/	*n.*	人员组合，投资组合
stakeholder	/ˈsteɪkhəʊldə(r)/	*n.*	股东，享有股份或利润的人
catalog	/ˈkætəlɒg/	*v.*	被列在一个目录中，编制……的目录
pay off			取得好结果，获得成功
lose out			不成功，受损失
roll in			滚滚而来，大量涌来
Wall Street			华尔街（纽约的金融中心）
ROI			投资回报（return on investment）

I. Listen to the conversation and choose the best answers to the questions you hear.

1. A. Marketing themselves to a variety of audiences.

   B. Marketing their companies to Wall Street investors.

   C. Marketing their products and services to customers.

   D. Marketing their overall corporate brand to the public.

2. A. CEOs should spend this critical period of time examining overall market conditions.

   B. CEOs should spend this critical period of time communicating with their employees.

   C. CEOs should spend this critical period of time enhancing their corporate image.

   D. CEOs should spend this critical period of time keeping in touch with local governments and mass media.

3. A. CEO's speeches and presentations are listed on some company websites.

   B. Internet has become an important marketing tool for CEOs themselves.

   C. Most CEOs use their companies' websites as their personal home pages.

   D. CEOs use the Internet to gain instant access to their staff and customers.

4. A. When a company nominates its new CEO.

   B. When a company is involved in rumors and crises.

   C. When a company releases its annual financial report.

   D. When a company launches its new range of products.

5. A. Internet will exert greater influence on CEOs and change their attitudes toward marketing.

   B. Modern CEOs will take more interest in marketing their products and themselves via the Internet.

   C. More CEOs will have marketing backgrounds and better understand the significance of good marketing.

D. Online marketing will become more and more popular and bring huge earnings for companies in the future.

II. Listen to the conversation again and decide whether the following statements are true or false. Write T for true and F for false in the brackets.

1. (   ) *Ceogo.com* is a website founded to deal with news and information about management and marketing.

2. (   ) Generally CEOs are more concerned with marketing their products, services and overall corporate brand.

3. (   ) Far more Fortune 500 CEOs have their backgrounds in finance and operations than in marketing and sales.

4. (   ) CEOs tomorrow must acquire more marketing skills as they will be solely responsible for corporate communications.

5. (   ) CEOs are advised to spend their first 100 days listening earnestly to customers and earning their trust and respect.

6. (   ) It's critical for new CEOs to market themselves internally because employee support is essential to their success.

7. (   ) Most companies do a good job of website managing as they consider the Web an important reputation-management tool.

8. (   ) When companies are in the hot seat, media and financial analysts often visit their company websites for information.

9. (   ) Many CEOs stay in their positions for a relatively short period of time, while the results of marketing tend to be long term.

10. (   ) Marketing staff will have a better time in the future because more CEOs will consider recruiting employees with marketing experience.

Passage

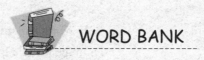

WORD BANK

ingrained	/ɪnˈgreɪnd/	*a.*	根深蒂固的
predominant	/prɪˈdɒmɪnənt/	*a.*	占主导地位的，（在数量、技术、地位等上）占优势的
masculine	/ˈmæskjʊlɪn/	*a.*	男人的，男子气概的
chagrin	/ˈʃægrɪn/	*n.*	懊恼，气愤
resemblance	/rɪˈzembləns/	*n.*	相似，类同之处
proscribe	/prəʊˈskraɪb/	*v.*	禁止
objectionable	/əbˈdʒekʃənəbl/	*a.*	引起反对的
Muslim	/ˈmuzlɪm/	*n.*	伊斯兰教徒，穆斯林
Allah	/ˈælə/	*n.*	（伊斯兰教的）真主
Islam	/ˈɪzlɑːm/	*n.*	伊斯兰教，伊斯兰教信徒
Islamic	/ɪzˈlæmɪk/	*a.*	伊斯兰的，伊斯兰教的
Bangladesh	/ˌbɑːŋgləˈdeʃ/	*n.*	孟加拉国
Indonesia	/ˌɪndəʊˈniːzjə/	*n.*	印度尼西亚
run afoul of			和……冲突，与……相抵触
purse strings			钱袋口上的绳子，金钱

I. Listen to the passage and choose the best answers to the questions you hear.

1. A. Red.   B. Blue.   C. Pink.   D. Yellow.

2. A. Nike intended to put the Arabic word for Allah on its footwear products.

   B. Nike included the Arabic word for Allah in its flame-design shoe logo.

   C. The poor quality of the Nike shoes drew protests from Muslim consumers.

   D. Muslims took offence at the likeness between the Nike shoe logo and the Arabic word for Allah.

3. A. Thom McAn is the first shoe manufacturer to put the word Allah on its products.

   B. Thom McAn is a shoe producer that fell in the same marketing trap as Nike did.

   C. Thom McAn intended to insult Muslims by putting the word Allah on its products.

   D. Thom McAn first used the flame-design logo that was considered objectionable to

Muslims.

4. A. In Africa.   B. In North America.

    C. In Southeast Asia.   D. In the Middle East.

5. A. Negligence of other cultural traditions will cause heavy losses for global marketers.

    B. Color associations such as blue is for boys and pink is for girls are instinctive.

    C. Much of the Islamic world associates yellow with females and red with males.

    D. Marketers must value Muslim traditions as Islam is the fastest-growing religion.

II. Listen to the passage again and answer the questions briefly according to what you hear.

1. What incurred protests from Muslims about Nike's products?

    _____

2. Why did Muslims feel insulted when they saw the Nike and Thom McAn shoe logos?

    _____

    _____

    _____

3. What is the most populous Islamic nation in the world? And how many Muslim citizens does it have?

    _____

4. What is thought to be offensive to Muslims?

    _____

    _____

5. What would be the consequence if marketers turn a blind eye to the traditions of other cultures?

    _____

6. What lesson can be learned from the Nike and Thom McAn cases?

    _____

    _____

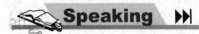 **Speaking** ▶▶

Discussion

☎ Work in pairs. Examine the Thom McAn shoe logo closely and tell your partner what you think of its graphic design.

☎ Work in groups. Nike, as one of the most famous sportswear brands in the world, is always actively engaged in various marketing practices. Discuss with your group and decide:

□ How is Nike doing in the market of China?

□ What marketing strategies does Nike adopt to promote its brand in the Chinese market?

□ Are Nike's marketing strategies effective and successful in China? Why or why not?

□ If you work for Nike, how would you market it more strongly in the Chinese market?

☎ Work as a class. Share your insights with the rest of the class.

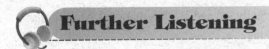

Short Recordings

WORD BANK

iconic	/aɪ'kɒnɪk/	*a.*	图标的，偶像的
topping	/'tɒpɪŋ/	*n.*	放在食品上的浇头，顶部，上层
pinch	/pɪntʃ/	*v.*	捏，挤，使苦恼，使萎缩
batter	/'bætə/	*v.*	猛击
burgeon	/'bɜːdʒən/	*v.*	迅速成长，发展
rebate	/'riːbeɪt/	*n.*	折扣，回扣
Minneapolis			明尼阿波利斯（美国城市）

I. In this section, you will hear five short recordings. For each piece, decide what action each company took or will take to boost its business.

1. J. M. Smucker	....	A. Cost reduction
2. Coca-Cola	....	B. Senior management change
3. Toys R Us	....	C. Company acquisition
4. General Motors	....	D. Brand expansion
5. Google	....	E. Service improvement
		F. Sales promotions
		G. Image enhancement
		H. Company restructuring

II. Listen to the five recordings again and decide whether the following statements are true or false. Write T for true and F for false in the brackets.

1. (　　) Jif peanut butter is a brand originally owned by International Multifoods Corp. and now purchased by Smucker.

2. (　　) Smucker anticipates the acquisition of International Multifoods Corp. will help it dominate the bakery industry.

3. (　　) Don Knauss, the newly appointed CEO, faces a tough challenge in reviving Coca-Cola's business in North America market.

4. (　　) Suffering from economic slowdown and fierce competition, Coca-Cola Co. has

cut more than 1,000 jobs in North America in the past year.

5. (   ) Toys R Us Inc., the New Jersey-based toy retailer, plans to put more emphasis on its weaker baby business.

6. (   ) Sales at its Babies R Us stores went up 3.6 percent although Toys R Us Inc. announced a 4.9 percent decrease in same-store sales at US toy stores during the key holiday period.

7. (   ) GM, the world's largest automaker, offered new sales incentives to stimulate demand after its US sales fell more than 15 percent in June.

8. (   ) Dealers are expecting GM to provide new cash rebates, cut lease payments and offer interest-free loans to further boost sales.

9. (   ) Google Inc. adopts service-enhancement strategy to prevent Internet users from turning to other Web search providers.

10. (   ) In order to attract more searchers, Google intends to integrate search technology with software development and media service.

Home Listening

Business News

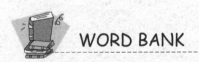

WORD BANK

backlash	/'bæklæʃ/	*n.*	强烈的反响，后冲力
legislation	/ˌledʒɪs'leɪʃən/	*n.*	立法，法规
outsourcing	/'aut.sɔːsɪŋ/		外部采办，外购（公司原自行制造的部件改向外国供应商订购）
liberalize	/'lɪbərəlaɪz/	*v.*	使自由化，使开明
the Philippines			菲律宾（亚洲东部的一个国家）
Israel			以色列（西南亚的一个国家）

Listen to the business news report and decide whether the following statements are true or false. Write T for true and F for false in the brackets.

1. (   )   People in Britain and the United States are more and more concerned about job losses to foreign countries.

2. (   )   India urges Asian countries to work out a common strategy to act against Western countries exploiting their cheap labor.

3. (   )   Western companies have been moving labor-intensive work to countries such as India, China and the Philippines to take advantage of unskilled cheap workforce there.

4. (   )   Multinational companies are transferring customer support work to Asian countries though they all locate their development centers in Western countries.

5. (   )   In order to protect local jobs, developed nations may make laws to restrict the flight of jobs into developing countries.

6. (   )   Organizations like WTO are places where both developed and developing nations seek to balance their respective interests through negotiation.

7. (   )   Outsourcing helps Asian companies raise production efficiency, reap more profits and thus create more growth opportunities.

8. (   )   Western companies are expected to cut back on the number of foreign employees under pressure from the labor unions.

Unit 15

Advertising

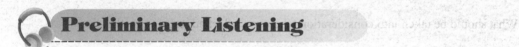

Preliminary Listening

Dictation

Listen to the following short paragraph and fill in the blanks with what you hear.

Advertising is the (1) _____ of a cause, idea, product, or service by an identified sponsor attempting to (2) _____

_____. Advertising has evolved to take a variety of forms and has permeated nearly (3) _____. Every major medium is used to deliver the message: (4) _____

_____. Advertisements can also be seen (5) _____

_____, on the walls of an airport walkway, and the sides of buses, or heard (6) _____ — nearly anywhere (7) _____

_____ can be placed. Advertising clients are predominantly, but not exclusively, for-profit corporations seeking to (8) _____

_____.

Listening & Speaking

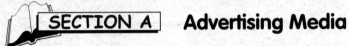

SECTION A Advertising Media

Pre-listening ▶▶

Discussion

Discuss the following questions with your partner and take notes when necessary.

1. What should be taken into consideration when you select advertising media?

----

2. What do you think of Internet as an advertising medium?

Listening ▶▶

Conversation

WORD BANK

symphony	/ˈsɪmfənɪ/	n.	交响乐，交响曲
underwrite	/ˌʌndəˈraɪt/	v.	承诺支付，认购，包销
assortment	/əˈsɔːtmənt/	n.	分类

billboard	/'bɪlbɔːd/	*n.*	（户外）广告牌
leaflet	/'liːflɪt/	*n.*	活页广告，传单
matchbook	/'mætʃbʊk/	*n.*	纸板火柴
metropolitan	/ˌmetrə'pɒlɪtən/	*a.*	大城市的，大都会的
proportionately	/prə'pɔːʃənɪtlɪ/	*ad.*	相称地，成比例地
justify	/'dʒʌstɪfaɪ/	*v.*	证明……有道理
toss	/tɒs/	*v.*	投，掷
impair	/ɪm'peə/	*v.*	削弱
subscribe to			捐款，捐助
Ford			福特汽车
General Motors (GM)			通用汽车
Chrysler			克莱斯勒汽车

I. Listen to the conversation and choose the best answers to the questions you hear.

1. A. Brand advertising.
   B. Comparative advertising.
   C. Primary-demand advertising.
   D. Institutional advertising.

2. A. "Raincoats are on-sale today at $9.95".
   B. "Welcome to Nestle Coffee Music Hour".
   C. "Milk, milk, natural food".
   D. "Ours is sugar-free".

3. A. Direct-action advertising.
   B. Institutional advertising.
   C. Primary-demand advertising.
   D. Comparative advertising.

4. A. Selectiveness.   B. Cheapness.
   C. Flexibility.   D. Effectiveness.

5. A. It does not reach the right audience they target.
   B. It goes beyond the advertising costs they can afford.
   C. It can not reach as wide an audience as newspaper advertising.
   D. It will not bring them the profit in proportion to their advertising expense.

II. Listen to the conversation again and complete the following notes with what you hear.

About Advertising

Types of advertising:

☐ Direction-action advertising
  ✓ (1) _____
  ✓ (2) _____
  ✓ (3) _____
☐ (4) _____

Variety of advertising media:

☐ Television, radio, newspaper, magazines
☐ (5) _____
☐ Specialty advertising
  e.g. (6) _____
☐ (7) _____
☐ (8) _____
☐ Direct mail
☐ (9) _____
☐ And others
  e.g. (10) _____

Selection of advertising media:

Questions to consider in selecting appropriate advertising media

☐ (11) _____
☐ (12) _____

Passage

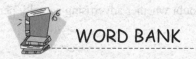

WORD BANK

campaign	/kæmˈpeɪn/	*n.*	（政治或商业性）活动
contend	/kənˈtend/	*v.*	主张
unjustified	/ʌnˈdʒʌstɪfaɪd/	*a.*	未被证明其正确的
availability	/əˌveɪləˈbɪlɪtɪ/	*n.*	可用性，有效性
inventory	/ˈɪnvəntərɪ/	*n.*	存货
subsidize	/ˈsʌbsɪdaɪz/	*v.*	资助，津贴
periodical	/ˌpɪərɪˈɒdɪkəl/	*n.*	期刊，杂志
panacea	/ˌpænəˈsɪə/	*n.*	万能药，灵丹妙药

I. Listen to the passage and choose the best answers to the questions you hear.

1. A. A large percentage of the consumers interviewed did not believe advertising always means what it says.

    B. The majority of the consumers interviewed were in favor of stricter government regulation over advertising.

    C. More than half of the consumers interviewed felt advertising is not as informative as it used to be.

    D. According to many consumers interviewed, advertising promises more than the product really delivers.

2. A. When newcomers have entered the field.

    B. When a new marketplace is developed.

    C. When market competition becomes intense.

    D. When a new line of products is launched.

3. A. Periodicals.   B. Newspapers.

    C. Outdoor billboards.   D. Commercial radios.

4. A. Newly released products.   B. Overcharged products.

C. Products of high quality.   D. Products with great demand.

5. A. Many experts argue against the accusation that advertising increases the costs.

   B. Advertising is most effective when it is used to sell a poor product or service.

   C. Advertising is successful in building brand loyalty and thus bringing the costs down.

   D. Quite a few people doubt whether advertising actually performs any useful informational functions.

II. Listen to the passage again and complete the notes with what you hear.

Public attitude towards advertising:
Among the consumers interviewed,

❑ more than 60 percent said advertising (1) _____.

❑ 58 percent believed advertising (2) _____.

❑ 61 percent felt advertising (3) _____.

Pros and cons of advertising:
Negative: Advertising increases costs

❑ (4) _____ push companies to sell products at higher prices.

❑ (5) _____ developed from expensive nationwide advertising campaigns makes it difficult for (6)_____; the consequent market domination enables a few large companies to (7)_____ _____ than they could in a more competitive situation.

Positive: Advertising reduces the unit cost

❑ Advertising stimulates demand and thus enables (8) _____ _____.

Informational functions of advertising:

❑ informing a potential buyer of (9) _____

❑ informing consumers in advance of (10) _____

❑ informing the customer (11) _____ or better than the competitor's

❑ subsidizing the media we rely on for (12) _____

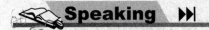 **Speaking** ▶▶|

Discussion

• •

Advertisers use various media to convey commercial messages to their target audiences. The question they are dying to ask is if their ads are reaching the right audience and generating the best response. Unfortunately, there is no simple answer. Understanding the advantages and disadvantages of major advertising media may be of great help.

☎ **Work in groups. Discuss with your group and work out what you perceive as the possible advantages and disadvantages of the following advertising media.**

Advertising Media	Advantages	Disadvantages
Newspaper		
Magazine		
Television		
Radio		
Direct Mail		
Outdoor Sign		
Internet		

☎ **Work as a class. Compare and share your findings with the rest of the class.**

SECTION B Advertising Techniques

Pre-listening ▶▶▶

Discussion

Discuss the following questions with your partner and take notes when necessary.

1. What do you think makes a good advertisement?

----

2. Do you think advertising should always mean what it claims? Why or why not?

Listening ▶▶▶

Conversation

WORD BANK

gear	/gɪə(r)/	v.	使适应，使适合
flyer	/ˈflaɪə/	n.	（广告）传单
demographic	/ˌdeməˈgræfɪk/	a.	人口的，人口统计学的
release	/rɪˈliːs/	v.	发表，发布

I. Listen to the conversation and choose the best answers to the questions you hear.

1. A. 1.   B. 2.   C. 3.   D. 10.

2. A. They know what prices are affordable to their customers.

   B. They know how their customers obtain their information.

   C. They know what products appeal to their customers most.

   D. They know how they are going to market to their customers.

3. A. The type of your business.   B. The size of your business.

   C. The profitability of your business.   D. The advertising budget of your business.

4. A. TV.   B. Magazines.   C. Internet.   D. Fliers.

5. A. Internet advertising proves to be the most effective way for entrepreneurs to market their businesses.

   B. Young entrepreneurs are encouraged to base their marketing strategies on themselves when they are targeting teenagers.

   C. General ads are recommended by Ben because they appear on any website and they are less expensive.

   D. It varies from company to company as to how heavily to invest in marketing and advertising efforts.

II. Listen to the conversation again and answer the following questions with what you hear.

1. How old was Ben when he started his first business? And what kind of business is it?

   _____

   _____

2. What does Ben see as the main advertising mistake young entrepreneurs are repeatedly making?

   _____

   _____

3. According to Ben, how do teenagers usually get their information?

   _____

   _____

4. According to Ben, how can young entrepreneurs avoid doing blind ads?

   _____

   _____

5. When young entrepreneurs market to their peers, why are they warned against basing

their strategies too much on themselves?

_____

_____

6. When should a consumer company commit a large proportion of its budget to marketing and advertising?

_____

_____

7. Why is Internet advertising said to be the most effective way for young entrepreneurs to market their businesses?

_____

_____

8. What does Ben suggest if a lot of people are visiting your site but not buying?

_____

_____

_____

Passage

WORD BANK

puff	/pʌf/	*n.*	吹嘘，宣传广告
		v.	吹捧
spot	/spɒt/	*v.*	认出，发现
mouthwash	/ˈmaʊθwɒʃ/	*n.*	漱口水
panther	/ˈpænθə/	*n.*	美洲豹（此处用作品牌名）
sparkle	/ˈspɑːkl/	*n.*	闪光，光彩（此处用作品牌名）
burger	/ˈbɜːgə/	*n.*	碎肉夹饼
rim	/rɪm/	*n.*	边，缘

I. Listen to the passage and answer the following questions with what you hear.

1. What is the passage mainly about?

   _____

   _____

2. What is the characteristic of advertising puffs?

   _____

   _____

3. Can the manufacturer say anything about its products? Why or why not?

   _____

   _____

4. What are "image-making" advertisements?

   _____

   _____

5. What is the actual body size of a frozen pie labeled as "nine-inch pie" in the supermarket?

   _____

   _____

6. How should we measure a pie if we want to know its actual body size?

   _____

   _____

II. Listen to the conversation again and complete the notes with what you hear.

Advertising Puffs

Ways of protection from misleading ads:
- ❑ FTC regulates the content of advertisements and decides on:
  - (1) _____
- ❑ Individual consumer can protect himself from misleading ads by:
  - (2) _____

Types of advertising puffs:
- ❑ (3) _____
- ❑ (4) _____
- ❑ (5) _____

Ways to spot advertising puffs by questioning:
- ☐ (6) _____
- ☐ (7) _____
- ☐ (8) _____

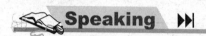

Speaking ▷▷▷

Discussion

☎ **Work in pairs. Below is a list of advertising slogans along with brand names in random order. Discuss with your partner and match the slogans to the appropriate brands.**

Slogans	Brands
(j) Don't ask why, try Bud Dry.	a. McDonalds
(c) Ask For More.	b. Kentucky Fried Chicken
(f) E-business solutions.	c. Pepsi
(k) Maybe she's born with it — maybe it's Maybelline.	d. Nike
(o) The Freshmaker!	e. Head & Shoulders (shampoo)
(l) Have a break, have a Kit Kat.	f. IBM
(i) Betcha can't eat just one.	g. BMW
(d) Just do it.	h. United Airlines
(e) I never knew you had dandruff.	i. Lays
(g) Sheer driving pleasure.	j. Budweiser
(h) Fly the friendly skies.	k. Maybelline (makeup)
(m) The happiest place on Earth.	l. Kit Kat candy
(a) I'm lovin' it.	m. Disneyland
(b) Finger lickin' good.	n. Maxwell House (coffee)
(n) Good to the last drop.	o. Mentos (candy)

☎ **Work in groups. Pick out a slogan you like best from the above list and explain to the rest of the group why it is your favorite. The following tips are for your reference.**

A Slogan Should:	A Slogan Should NOT:
📁 Be memorable	📁 Be in current use by others
📁 Include a key benefit	📁 Prompt a sarcastic or negative response
📁 Differentiate the brand	📁 Be pretentious
📁 Impart positive feelings for the brand	📁 Be negative
📁 Reflect the brand's personality	📁 Make you say "So what?" or "Ho-hum"
📁 Be competitive	📁 Make you say "Oh yeah?"
📁 Be original	📁 Be meaningless
📁 Be simple	📁 Be complicated or clumsy
📁 Be neat	📁 ...
📁 Be believable	
📁 ...	

Further Listening

Short Recordings

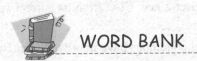

WORD BANK

franchisee	/ˌfræntʃaɪˈziː/	*n.*	特许经销代理人
dog	/dɒg/	*v.*	紧紧缠住，使苦恼
anemic	/əˈniːmɪk/	*a.*	无力的，缺乏活力的

tax	/tæks/	*v.*	使负重担，使受压力
conviction	/kən'vɪkʃən/	*n.*	判决有罪，定罪
contention	/kən'tenʃən/	*n.*	论点
penchant	/pɒŋ'ʃɒŋ; pentʃənt/	*n.*	强烈的倾向，爱好
shake-up	/'ʃeɪkʌp/	*n.*	重组，剧变
franchise	/'fræntʃaɪz/	*n.*	专卖权，经销权，特许经销
Morgan Stanley			摩根士丹利银行（以其优秀的金融咨询服务和市场执行实力享誉全球）
Winterhur			温特图尔（瑞士城市）

I. In this section, you will hear five short recordings. For each piece, decide why the chief of each company resigned or will resign from his position.

1. Burger King	....	A. Criminal record
2. Coca-Cola	....	B. Management reorganization
3. Smith & Wesson	....	C. Accounting fraud
4. Hollinger	....	D. Armed robberies
5. Credit Suisse	....	E. Corporate internal strife
		F. Conflict with the board
		G. Defalcation practices
		H. Substandard performance

II. Listen to the five recordings again and choose the best answers to the questions you hear.

1. A. Burger King Corp. is a huge hamburger chain ranking only second to McDonald's.

   B. Burger King would select a new CEO from its current senior management after Brad Blum's resignation.

   C. Burger King's financial conditions have improved after Brad Blum became its CEO in January of 2003.

   D. One fifth of Burger King's about 7,900 restaurants are reported to be losing money in recent years.

2. A. To avoid government investigation.

   B. To revive its sales and stock performance.

   C. To control its operations in North American market.

   D. To compete against its major rival, Pepsi Co. Inc.

3. A. James Joseph Minder was imprisoned for as long as 15 years in the 1950s and 1960s.

   B. Smith & Wesson attempted to conceal its chairman's criminal past before the newspaper report came out.

   C. James Joseph Minder would spend his time trying to help kids after his resignation.

   D. James Joseph Minder felt frustrated when his criminal past was revealed to the public.

4. A. Collecting improper payment.   B. Altering corporate records.

   C. Claiming disputed compensation.   D. Pushing the ex-CEO into resigning.

5. A. Management shake-up.   B. Corporate power struggle.

   C. His penchant to cut costs.   D. Pressure from the board.

Home Listening

Business News

WORD BANK

conglomerate	/kənˈglɒmərɪt/	n.	集团企业，联合大企业
meltdown	/ˈmeltdaʊn/	n.	彻底垮台，融化（过程）
aftermath	/ˈɑːftəmæθ/	n.	结果，后果
crack down on			制裁，镇压
level off			达到稳定，（使）变得平整
chaebol			韩国财阀，韩国大企业
off balance sheet			资产负债表外，账外
Duke University			杜克大学（美国著名的私立大学，位于北卡罗来纳州的达勒姆）
Hyundai			韩国现代集团（以建筑、造船、汽车行业为主，兼营钢铁、机械、贸易、运输、水泥生产、冶金、金融、电子工业等几十个行业的综合性企业集团）

Samsung	韩国三星集团（韩国最大的企业集团，业务涉及电子、金融、机械、化学等众多领域）
Daewoo	韩国大宇集团（韩国第二大企业集团，旗下大宇汽车公司系韩国第二大汽车生产企业）
LG	韩国LG集团（业务涉及化学、能源、通信、服务、电子制造等领域）
SK	韩国SK集团（以能源化工和信息通讯两大支柱产业为核心，系韩国第三大企业集团）

Listen to the business news report and decide whether the following statements are true or false. Write T for true and F for false in the brackets.

1. (   ) Barry Wood attributed South Korea's late 1990s financial crisis to the reckless financial dealings of the chaebols.

2. (   ) According to Edward Graham, a business professor at Duke University, the chaebols are still too powerful despite significant reform in some areas.

3. (   ) The new South Korean president has promised to reform the country's financial system to save the chaebols from going bankrupt.

4. (   ) After the 1997 crisis, Hyundai, Samsung, LG, and SK are the only conglomerates which still remain in business.

5. (   ) Off balance sheet operations are responsible for the breakdown of the Enron energy trading company in Texas.

6. (   ) South Korea has followed the example of China and fully opened its economy to foreign direct investment.

7. (   ) The chaebols in South Korea are blamed for reckless financial dealings and illegal securities transactions.

8. (   ) South Korea's economy recorded impressive economic growth rates in the 1980s and early 1990s.

9. (   ) After the financial crisis, South Korean economy shrank from ten percent annual growth to eight percent in 1998.

10. (   ) It was not until 5 years later that South Korea's economy started to recover from the 1997 economic recession.